TRUE CRIME : MARYLAND

TRUE CRIME : MARYLAND

The State's Most Notorious Criminal Cases

Ed Okonowicz

STACKPOLE
BOOKS

Published by
STACKPOLE BOOKS
5067 Ritter Road
Mechanicsburg, PA 17055
www.stackpolebooks.com

Printed in the United States of America

10 9 8 7 6 5 4 3 2 1

FIRST EDITION

Cover design by Caroline M. Stover and Tessa J. Sweigert

Cover photos: Serrated pocket knife, ©Lawrence Manning/Corbis; William Brad-ford Bishop wanted posters and John Allen Muhammad mugshots, Montgomery County Sheriff's Office; $5,000 reward poster, Ann Arrundell County Historical Society; hanging and Thanos headline, Historical Society of Cecil County

Library of Congress Cataloging-in-Publication Data

Okonowicz, Ed, 1947–
    True crime : Maryland : the state's most notorious criminal cases /
  Ed Okonowicz. — 1st ed.
      p.   cm.
  Includes bibliographical references.
  ISBN-13: 978-0-8117-3603-9 (pbk.)
  ISBN-10: 0-8117-3603-2 (pbk.)
    1. Crime—Maryland—History—Case studies. 2. Murder—Maryland—History—Case studies. 3. Maryland—History. I. Title.
HV6793.M3O56   2009
364.152'30922752—dc22

                                                 2009003267

Contents

Introduction

Many people are fascinated with crime. In fact, the more sensational the offense, the more eagerly they follow the case. The same applies to trial and punishment. Present grisly or graphic evidence and announce a severe or deadly sentence, and the ever-curious public will savor every gruesome detail.

My interest in true crime started when I witnessed an execution while working on an article for a regional magazine. The unusual experiences associated with this assignment began on a winter night in 1996, just before midnight. I was in an administration building of the Delaware Correctional Institution in Smyrna, a small town in the middle of a small state. Along with nearly one hundred other correspondents—representing publications and broadcast news outlets from across the country, plus a film crew that had traveled to the rural Delaware village from Europe—I sat and waited. The hours passed slowly as each of us clutched a small, blue, bake-sale-style raffle ticket. We were eager to learn the results of a drawing that would name the late-night gathering's eight "winners." The prize: admittance into the state's execution chamber to witness the last legal hanging in the United States.

With nothing much to do in the former school gymnasium, I spent time studying the crowd's diverse members, all waiting and wandering around the stark, uncomfortable room. In the rear of the hall, television news anchors primped for the camera. They concentrated on adjusting their hair and perfecting their makeup before they read "this-just-in" updates, "direct from the hanging scene."

Less concerned with their looks were the veteran newspaper reporters, scattered on uncomfortable metal chairs throughout the hall. A few—representing papers from New York City ("the city," they said to the rest of us, as if there is only one) and Washington, D.C.—wore expensive suits and spoke in a haughty tone. They sighed and glanced unpleasantly around at the surroundings, complaining loudly about the lack of luck that had placed them on the deathwatch vigil in, of all places, "Nowhere, Delaware."

But none of the moaners dared leave the premises, lest they miss the results of the Maxwell House coffee-can drawing, when a state corrections official would reach in the container and select the matching ends of the ticket stubs held by the lucky few.

Unfortunately, that Wednesday night my number wasn't called. Along with more than ninety other losers, I waited several more hours in the hall, anticipating the return of the chosen few who had witnessed the prison death scene. About 1:30 A.M., I listened to a panel of my "luckier" colleagues, who sat behind microphones in the front of the hall and offered their impressions of murderer Billy Bailey's state-sanctioned necktie party. In detail, they described his march up the rustic, twenty-three-step, wooden gallows; the hooded executioner's placement of the noose; the noise accompanying the body's sudden drop through the scaffold's trapdoor; and the slow twirling of the corpse as it dangled from the thick, tightly stretched rope. Like the others in the audience, I took notes for my upcoming article.

But luck and persistence paid off five evenings later. The following Monday night, I sat in the same room, clutching another blue ticket stub. I had returned to Smyrna for Delaware's next scheduled execution. You might say the First State was offering an execution "twofer" that month. Not surprisingly, the number of media representatives attending that night's featured event—a more common lethal injection—had dwindled significantly. Less than three dozen reporters had bothered to come back to the converted-gymnasium waiting room to report on the drug-induced death of the next convicted murderer.

Just before midnight, my number was called. I had won the opportunity to enter into the prison's sterile death chamber to witness the execution of murderer William Flamer. Through a large glass wall, we observed the killer's long-awaited demise. But unlike the brutal death of Flamer's unfortunate victims, the end of this murderer's life was as peaceful and painless as a baby falling to sleep. "Death Watch," my on-the-scene report of the two evenings, appeared a few months later in *Delaware Today* magazine. Even though more than a decade has passed, I am able to recall vividly the memories of those two nights, probably because the experiences were rare, unusual, and associated with murderers who had committed horrific crimes, both in 1979.

Billy Bailey was executed by hanging for shooting an elderly couple in their home in a small village. The husband was eighty, the wife seventy-three. Bailey was on a prison work-release program at the time of the murders. Because he had been convicted of the crimes while hanging had still been a legal method of punishment in Delaware, Bailey was offered the choice of dying that way or by lethal injection, which had been instituted since his conviction. He chose hanging, and it was carried out according to his wishes.

William Flamer was executed by lethal injection for the brutal killings of his elderly uncle and aunt. Upset they would not turn over their Social Security check so he could continue a drinking binge, he stabbed them more than 150 times with a bayonet and a kitchen paring knife.

Certainly, the number of stories, size of headlines, and amount of front-page space given to articles in the days following sensational crimes and during their eventual trials demonstrate the public's fascination with and hunger for the lurid details. "There's nothing that gets the juices flowing in any town like a good murder," I read many years ago in a popular crime novel. Though I'm unable to offer proper attribution, the author's fictional character stated a fact that's been verified endlessly since biblical times.

Criminal behavior often generates horrific images and stimulates the imagination of readers, viewers, and listeners. Newspaper and magazine publishers, as well as radio and television station owners, follow the same proven principle: The grislier the crime, the larger the headline or the longer the airtime.

If handled properly and delivered quickly, crime fattens the bottom line. It's the equivalent of retailers' Black Friday. And because of the large number of the unlawful in our society, crime is not a once-a-year event. Its frequency allows criminal acts to be packaged, spotlighted, and marketed continuously. Murders, robberies, kidnappings, riots, disappearances, and drug overdoses sell at the newsstand, cause lines to form at the box office, and fill sofas in front of living-room televisions. The latest killing or drug bust isn't on page 16, competing for attention with local school-board or zoning hearing announcements. A fresh murder or big-money robbery— preferably with blood and injuries—hits readers between the eyes like a wet snowball, in the form of bold, black, extra large headlines above the fold on page 1.

Insatiable viewers and savvy advertisers are responsible for a never-ending series of programs such as the hit shows *Law & Order* and *CSI*. Though professional writers create much of the dialogue in these programs, a number of plots and characters are based on real-life events. Former police officers, prosecutors, and in some cases, even convicted criminals serve as paid consultants, providing realistic details to ensure accuracy. Crime is good, but true crime is better—unless you happen to be a victim.

That said, this book is a look at only a small number of the more sensational crimes or unusual transgressions that occurred in the state of Maryland. A comprehensive examination would fill enough volumes to rival a set of encyclopedias. Each of the state's county law enforcement units could provide at least half a dozen cases worthy of inclusion. With hundreds of murders taking place each year within the jurisdiction of Baltimore, several volumes could be devoted to senseless acts of violence that have occurred in that major city alone. And in every rural and urban locale, crimes continue to be committed.

But authors have to start—and finish—somewhere. While researching this project, I found that my being somewhat of a pack rat proved worthwhile. One of the traits many writers share is a tendency to save news clippings of what they think at the time are interesting stories. Often these newspaper or magazine articles merely catch the eye, serving no immediate purpose. Nevertheless, we place them aside for future reading, with the thought that they might come in handy someday.

On the last day of the recent millennium, December 31, 1999, I had dropped an Associated Press story by writer Kathy Gambrell into a manila folder. Other than the headline—"Some of Maryland's most notorious crimes: List of crimes compiled by Maryland members of the Associated Press"—the article remained unread until December 2007, when I rescued it from the bottom of a growing stack of other yellowed clippings long ago saved for "future use."

In her introduction, Gambrell wrote: "Following is a list of the most notable Maryland crimes this century based on a poll of Maryland broadcast and newspaper members of the Associated Press. The list, which is chronological, is by no means a complete record of criminal acts."

My thanks are extended to those who participated in that informal poll nearly a decade ago; several of their selections are included as chapters in this book. But this limited number of stories offers only a glimpse of the long and varied history of crime, punishment, and criminals—captured, imprisoned, released, executed, or still at large—in the Old Line State.

CHAPTER 1

A Brief History of
Crime in Maryland

***

To understand the crimes committed and punishments adminis-tered throughout Maryland since its settlement, it is important to be aware that judicial and public safety attitudes have been affected by the state's his-tory and geography—and this remains the case today.

From Maryland's settlement in 1634 to its important present-day location adjacent to the nation's capital, events—and in this par-ticular case, the nature of many crimes—have been influenced by the state's critical role as a mid-Atlantic crossroads of the young American nation. Especially important are the countries of origin and religious preferences of Maryland's earliest settlers, its occu-pational and cultural identity associated with the Chesapeake Bay, and finally, its territorial importance and significant involvement in our nation's early wars, particularly the Revolution, War of 1812, and Civil War.

* * *

Maryland is classified as a border state. Located both south and west of the Mason-Dixon line—which symbolically divides the country's northern and southern regions—the Old Line State, politically, has always fallen into a geographic gray zone. During the Civil War, the state was listed as siding with the North, but its citizens exhibited divided loyalties. A significant number of its residents and leading politicians advocated Confederate causes, such as slavery, states' rights, and distrust of a powerful Federal authority. Because of its central location and valuable Chesapeake Bay water routes, Robert E. Lee's rebel troops and Yankee units under a succession of commanders considered Maryland a valuable prize. During the four years of bloody conflict, both Northern and Southern armies used the state like an interstate highway, tromping over its mountains and through its fields and sailing along its waterways.

But Maryland's important role as a border-state crossroads had begun decades earlier. Immediately after the passage of the Slave Trade Act of 1808, which prohibited the importation of slaves into this country, enterprising Maryland night riders or slave catchers rounded up and kidnapped slaves who had previously escaped or had bought their freedom. These latter individuals, called freemen, were coveted human prizes. After being kidnapped, they were kept prisoner on Maryland properties—usually located near waterways leading to the Chesapeake Bay—until it was safe for them to be sold back into bondage to enterprising slave traffickers who had sailed secretly into Maryland from the Deep South. Plantation owners, who needed a steady supply of cheap labor to replenish their dwindling workforce, eagerly awaited the delivery of this officially banned human cargo.

In the decades immediately preceding the Civil War, Marylander Harriet Tubman helped establish the Underground Railroad, a secretive network of "conductors" that guided slave "passengers" to freedom. Her web of hidden routes and safe houses, known as "stations," helped free hundreds of slaves, and the publicity surrounding her success helped lay the groundwork for the eventual abolition of slavery.

But it would take more than one hundred years for the full effects of Tubman's efforts to come to a climax, with the civil rights demonstrations of the 1960s. Up until that time, Maryland and her sister states in the Deep South had moved slowly to grant full rights to African American citizens. Many former Confederate states maintained their separate-but-equal traditions, which were practiced in such public places as movie theaters, churches, schools, restaurants, swimming pools, and lunch counters. In the mid-twentieth century, scholars suggested that civil disobedience and riots demanding dramatic change and racial equality could be traced back to the persistence and bravery of Tubman, an illiterate slave from Dorchester County in southern Maryland.

In the early years of the state's settlement, New World settlers followed the seventeenth-century approaches to crime and punishment that had been practiced in England. This was to be expected, as citizens, church leaders, and political officials were familiar with these accepted methods, such as the pillory, stocks, whipping post, ducking stool, gossip bridle, iron cages, and branding iron. Such punishments were applied to criminals judged responsible for a range of crimes, ranging from public disturbances, not attending church services, and idle gossip to robbery, assault, and murder. Even more drastic and immediate methods were taken if a citizen happened to be accused of witchcraft.

In 1654, the misnamed ship *Charity* left England bound for Maryland's shore. A sudden and extended storm led the captain to believe a witch might be aboard. He enlisted the help of a passenger with ministerial credentials, and upon examining all of the vessel's women, they found one bearing an "unclean mark," indicating her association with the devil. To solve their stormy problem and dispose of the evil passenger, by now branded as a witch, the crew hanged Mary Lee from the tallest mast and tossed her "possessed" body into the sea as a sacrificial offering. When the storm suddenly stopped, all aboard agreed they had selected the correct passenger and taken the proper action to resolve their mutual plight.

Not altogether surprisingly, many colonies imported convicted criminals to boost the numbers of the settlement's limited workforce. In March 1739, 115 felons and convicts were taken from London's Newgate Prison and placed on the ship *York*, bound for Maryland. One wonders how many of these passengers of questionable background continued their criminal careers in the Maryland colony.

Colonial jailhouses were the responsibility of each individual county. Many were so poorly constructed—often nothing more than

CAT-O'-NINE-TAILS

Whipping, a sensational form of punishment administered before a crowd of rowdy bystanders, had been accepted in Maryland for centuries. Over time, however, its application was modified, restricted, and eventually written off the books—showing how changing public attitudes, political decisions, and the natural evolution of the field of criminology have affected the treatment of criminals in the state's penal system.

Being subjected to the lash in a public square was a common punishment in England during the Middle Ages. When settlers arrived in the New World, this was one of many sentences commonly accepted at the time. Not surprisingly, it became part of the newly formed justice system in many of the young colonies.

In an article titled "Colonial Crimes and Punishments," James A. Cox wrote: "Whipping sentences usually stipulated that the stripes be 'well laid on,' as the phrase went. In one case of a multiple whipping, the beadle—a minor church official—was ordered to lay on, but was so light-handed the sheriff seized the lash and scourged him, too, before turning to the prisoners. Bystanders gave the sheriff three cheers for his attention to duty."

an open pen where the captive was chained or watched—that the local constable had to remain at the site for extended periods to guard his prisoners. If the accused managed to escape, the constable was fined for poor execution of his duties. Death by hanging was a common practice in counties throughout the colony. Public executions on the gallows, in town squares or prison yards, were viewed as entertainment events and attracted massive crowds. These public spectacles continued to occur, to the delight of eager viewers, into the early twentieth century.

In 1882, Maryland established a new law authorizing the use of the whipping post as a punishment for wife beating. This statute directed law enforcement representatives to administer a designated

Whipping posts claimed a prominent place in colonial-era town squares and churchyards, usually standing beside the stocks and pillories.

In 1897, a *New York Times* reprint of an article from *The Cosmopolitan* stated: "The pillory, which usually accompanied the whipping of criminals, was regarded as a species of public entertainment. The rabble evidence such pleasure in pelting the culprits with eggs, vegetables and clods that Watson, in his historical annals of Philadelphia, declares that, inasmuch as the punishments were inflicted only on market days, the price of eggs was then systematically higher than common."

In New England, the lash was applied for the slightest offenses, such as sleeping during a sermon, dozing off at work, or kissing one's wife on a public street on a Sunday. Simply because of their religion, Quakers living in the northernmost New World colonies were marked as targets of public whippings. Initially, Maryland approved of the laying on of the lash for those committing more serious crimes—such as forgery, theft, Sabbath breaking, and blasphemy.

In 1882, Maryland generated new interest in use of the whipping post by passing a law authorizing its use for those found guilty of wife beating.

(continued on page 6)

An 1895 *New York Times* article noted the border state's successful use of the punishment to curtail domestic violence. The Maryland law stated: "Any person who shall brutally assault and beat his wife shall be deemed guilty of a misdemeanor, and upon presentment and conviction thereof by any court of competent jurisdiction, shall be sentenced to be whipped not exceeding forty lashes or be imprisoned for a term not exceeding one year, or both, in the discretion of the court."

When a Baltimore court sentenced a prisoner to a whipping, it caused a "big sensation, and the prisoner after his whipping corroborated the practical results of the law by saying that he never would make himself subject to the penalty again, and by declaring that the disgrace of it was worse than the physical discomforts. Since the law went into effect, cases of wife beating have been less numerous than formerly," the New York paper reported.

In 1896, John Boots of Chesapeake City, Maryland, was sentenced to ten lashes with the cat-o'-nine-tails, as the whip was nicknamed, for brutally beating his wife, Mary Boots. "About seventy-five people congregated

number of lashes on the back of the accused, often in a public setting. The form of punishment lasted until the mid-twentieth century (see sidebar).

Sometimes, however, crimes were committed and justice dispensed with the perpetrators knowing there was no possibility of capture or of being brought into courtrooms before white-wigged judges. Maryland's extensive coastline, which borders the Atlantic Ocean and surrounds the majority of the massive Chesapeake Bay, hosted an extensive shipbuilding industry. When builders weren't making large warships for the country's navy, these craftsmen were constructing watermen's workboats for fishing, clamming, oystering, hunting, and shipping.

Centuries ago, from Baltimore's Fells Point to its current-day tourist-popular Inner Harbor, large warehouses surrounded busy in the jail yard as witnesses, much to the dissatisfaction of Boots, who desired that no one be admitted. He also made a request that no one be allowed to take his picture while undergoing his humiliating punishment."

As criminal justice evolved during the twentieth century, whippings became less frequent. Cecil County made use of the lash for the final time in December 1940, when a wife beater was sentenced to sixty days in jail and "10 lashes on the bare back." In 1945, a Prince George's County man was sentenced to ten lashes, applied to the lower back. Roger B. Farquhar reported in the *Washington Post* that "a whip that had been a family heirloom since Civil War days was loaned for the occasion. Witnesses said the convicted wife-beater bit his lip so hard blood was seen on his mouth." In 1953, the Maryland legislature repealed the law allowing the whipping post to be used as punishment for any crime.

To the surprise of many, Maryland's next-door neighbor Delaware kept its whipping post—nicknamed "Red Hannah"—on the books until 1972, although the last criminal in that state was whipped—for beating a woman—in 1952.

wharves. In numerous saloons, brothels, and gambling houses on streets that lined the docks, people were often "shanghaied"—kidnapped and dragged aboard vessels heading out to sea—to serve as crewmembers. By the time they regained consciousness, the ship was far from land. The unfortunate victim had no choice but to accept the forced captivity and work as a member of the crew until the ship arrived at the next port. Unfortunately, some of these hijacked sailors never again set foot on land. They were paid "by the boom," a reference to their being tossed or knocked overboard by a swinging wooden beam before the ship approached port, thus allowing the captain and regular crew to divide the drowned victim's wages.

In 1807, the College of Medicine of Maryland was established as one of the first medical schools in the country. This learned institution also earned a reputation as a center of the country's grave-robbing industry. Located in Baltimore, this medical college's faculty physicians paid the school's janitorial staff to exhume freshly deceased bodies from nearby cemeteries and bring them back to the college for autopsies and classroom medical examinations, which were illegal at the time.

One administrator at the University of Maryland's Alumni Association office described the clandestine network and grave robbers' techniques as "incredible," saying, "It would have made today's drug smugglers look like children." Documents indicate that Maryland medical college faculty supplied bodies to schools as far away as New England for research and dissection. The "subjects," as they were referenced in an 1830 letter from a physician at the College of Medicine to a teaching colleague at Maine's Bowdoin College, were to be "put up in barrels of whiskey" for preservation during shipment and transport. "I shall immediately invoke Frank, our body snatcher (a better man never lifted a spade), and confer with him on the matter," the physician wrote. "We can get them without any difficulty at present, but I would not tell the world that any but ourselves should know that I have winked at their being sent out of state."

Over time, those criminal acts have become the source of new terminology. Some Baltimore tour guides and historians suggest that the school's grave-robbing techniques may have contributed to the familiar barroom term "rotgut whiskey," still used today when referring to cheap or foul-tasting liquor. Frequently, deteriorating snatched corpses would be lined up outside the college's Anatomical Hall awaiting study. To preserve these recently departed, stolen specimens, the corpses were stuffed into wooden barrels filled with cheap liquor. After the body was extracted from its temporary storage vat, the remaining soiled spirits were sold at a cheap price to unsuspecting college students or savvy proprietors of nearby saloons, who passed them on to their less discriminating patrons.

It was not until the late nineteenth century that laws in Maryland and other states were changed, legalizing the use of dead bodies—mainly of the homeless and criminals—for medical research.

Other early incidents of crime and lawlessness took place among those whose livelihoods depended on taking advantage of the state's natural resources. Along the Chesapeake Bay, market hunters trapped and shot waterfowl. As a matter of course, these rural sportsmen killed large numbers of game that far exceeded the legal limit, while always staying several steps ahead of state and federal game wardens. Oystermen, who also made their living on the bay and shallow waters, often became involved in territorial disputes over the waterways' limited natural resources. These conflicts—known as the "Oyster Wars"—sometimes turned deadly, pitting the bay harvesters against lawmen and setting watermen from Maryland against their counterparts in Virginia.

* * *

Along the state's Eastern Shore—the nine counties located east of the Chesapeake Bay—and to a degree in some of the state's western counties, enraged gangs called lynch mobs "solved" certain crimes, which they believed were committed by minorities, without a trial. From colonial days until the last public mob action in 1933, these groups illegally lynched, or hanged, African Americans accused of wrongdoing, not allowing the case to make it to court. Various estimates suggest that between twenty-nine and forty-two times, Maryland citizens broke into jails, dragged untried suspects through the streets, and strung them up in town squares or secluded forests. Lynchers, some dressed in their Sunday best, later posed beneath the dangling, mutilated bodies, as traveling postcard photographers or reporters captured the images for family albums and newspaper front pages.

Mob rule was not associated only with racial issues. In the days leading up to America's Revolution, Boston gained much fame for its well-known Tea Party in 1773. A mob of citizens dressed as Indians protested taxation without representation by dumping a shipload of British tea into the town harbor. A year later, in Maryland, they went even further. In Annapolis, the colony's capital, a mob tossed 2,300 pounds of the "detestable weed" overboard and set the ship on fire. The angry patriots also threatened to burn the shipowner's home to the ground, causing him to send his family back to England.

Some historians suggest that the first bloodshed of the Civil War occurred in Baltimore, Maryland's largest city and a hotbed of citizens proud of their Southern secessionist sympathies. Because of intense hatred for President Abraham Lincoln and reports of a suspected assassination attempt, the president-elect was forced to sneak through Baltimore on his way to the U.S. capital for his inauguration. Following the battle at Fort Sumter on April 12, 1861, anti-Union sentiment in the tense metropolis reached a fiery level.

When the first Union troops responding to Lincoln's call for volunteers arrived in Baltimore on their way to Washington, D.C., a mob formed. Since the Northern rail line did not go directly through Baltimore en route to Washington, the infantrymen of the 6th Massachusetts Regiment were forced to march through the city to a southbound station where their railcars were waiting. On April 19, 1861, as the young troops marched through town, a growing mob shouted threats at the soldiers and pelted them with bricks, stones, and heavy objects. The frightened Yankees fired into the crowd. When the panic was over, four Yankee soldiers and twelve Baltimore citizens had been killed in what became known as the Pratt Street Massacre or Pratt Street Riot.

Angry secessionists burned rail bridges north of the city to hamper the arrival of additional Union troops, and the Southerners also destroyed telegraph wires and poles, cutting off communication with Washington. Federal troops eventually occupied Baltimore, and *New York Tribune* editor Horace Greeley later wrote that the Maryland city where the riot occurred should be burned to the ground.

In a tale more appropriate to the Wild West, in January 1885, two masked bandits robbed train passengers at gunpoint along the rails spanning the Maryland-Pennsylvania border (Mason-Dixon line). In response, a posse of Philadelphia detectives traveled into northern

Maryland to apprehend members of the notorious Abe Buzzard gang, which they suspected of the crime. The culprits turned out, however, to be two local youths, who were captured without much fanfare or resistance. Enjoying the unusual criminal escapade, nearby Philadelphia newspapermen suggested there "was danger that Jesse James and all the western highwaymen . . . were advanced on the City of Brotherly Love."

In the 1920s, as a result of the nation's Prohibition laws restricting alcohol, farmers and western Maryland mountain folk earned much-needed income selling homemade moonshine whiskey, produced in family-operated stills. But more money was made by rumrunners in fast-moving boats that smuggled illegal spirits ashore along the hundreds of miles of Maryland ocean coastline and Chesapeake Bay shore. In *Chesapeake Rumrunners of the Roaring Twenties*, Eric Mills chronicles stories of illegal whiskey delivered by local and foreign craft along isolated coves. Certainly some of these operations involved cooperation among bribed law enforcement personnel and colorful bootleggers and speakeasy operators. Nevertheless, despite the destruction of thousands of illegal stills by revenue agents, the practice of brewing homemade moonshine liquor in the state persisted well into the 1950s, several decades after the nation's alcohol Prohibition laws were repealed.

A few Maryland crimes have gained national and, in some cases, even had international implications. In 1935, a rather comical incident occurred in the village of Elkton, located at the northeast corner of the state, along the road that served as a major thoroughfare through several eastern states. The prime player was a rural police chief, who thought he simply was doing his job when he arrested a well-dressed couple and their foreign-speaking chauffeur for speeding through his town. Unaware of the term "diplomatic immunity," the small-town constable handcuffed the minister from Persia and locked up the diplomat in the town jail. After the Maryland State Police located the missing official, it took the intervention of Cordell Hull, President Franklin Delano Roosevelt's secretary of state, to soothe the diplomat's ruffled feathers. But when news of the country-bumpkin-style arrest commanded several days of space on the front pages of the *Washington Post*, the diplomat's insulted home country broke off diplomatic relations with the United States.

In the latter half of the twentieth century, political corruption was so prevalent among county and high-profile state officials in Maryland that some observers commented that the state had earned the tarnished reputation as the second most corrupt in the nation, trailing only Louisiana. But the effects of these questionable practices did not end at the state line. Charges of tax evasion and bribery committed while holding the state's highest office followed former Maryland governor Spiro T. Agnew across the border into adjacent Washington. This caused the U.S. vice president under President Richard Nixon to plead *nolo contendre*, "no contest," to state charges of income tax evasion. In October 1973, after five years in office, Agnew resigned from a position where he sat only a heartbeat away from the presidency. Less than a year later, the Watergate scandal led President Richard Nixon to resign from office, and Gerald Ford, the man who had been appointed to fill Agnew's remaining term, took his place in the White House. Ford became the only man to serve as both vice president (by appointment) and president (by succession) of the United States without having been elected to either office.

* * *

The most well-known assassins in U.S. history are Lee Harvey Oswald and John Wilkes Booth. The latter, a northern Maryland native, was born in Bel Air, near the Mason-Dixon line. Conspiracy theorists frequently point out the uncanny similarities between the two shooters: Both killers went by three names with fifteen letters; Booth was born in 1839, Oswald in 1939; both men shot their subjects in the back of the head, on a Friday, in the presence of their victims' wives. Lincoln was killed in Ford's Theatre; Kennedy was killed in a Lincoln automobile, made by Ford. To this day, many still believe both men were part of much larger conspiracies and government cover-ups—especially since both assassins were killed while in custody, before they could be brought to trial and tell their stories in public.

After John Wilkes Booth's escape from Washington, D.C., he traveled through southern Maryland, benefiting from the assistance of fellow conspirators and a few unsuspecting citizens. Many of the locations where Booth stopped are indicated with state historical markers along a designated tourist route. But another site, in the center of Maryland not far from the nation's capital, hosts no formal marker of any kind. This busy shopping-center location was the site of an attempted assassination of another nationally known politician. And the shooting made front-page headlines across the nation during the American presidential primary race in 1972.

Following a speech in a shopping center parking lot in Laurel, Maryland, Arthur Bremer shot George Wallace, the governor of Alabama. The shooter had been stalking the Democratic presidential candidate for several months. Wallace survived the assassination attempt, and his assailant was convicted and sent to prison. Based on the surprising success of Wallace's earlier third-party presidential effort in 1968, some believe that had the governor not been shot, he would have had a significant impact on the outcome of the 1972 Democratic nomination and the party's platform. There also is speculation that Bremer's actions were conducted with at least some knowledge, and perhaps even limited support, of unnamed U.S. government agencies.

Like all careers, crime has changed with the times. New attitudes, laws, and products create new demands and new illegal opportunities. Canadian whiskey rumrunners, who landed on secluded beaches in the 1930s, have been replaced by today's drug smugglers, who tunnel under the Mexican–U.S. border. Others land small planes filled with illegal cargo in out-of-the-way fields and abandoned airports.

Technological advances have made knockoffs of name-brand products and illegally duplicated CDs and DVDs easier to produce than counterfeit currency.

Terms associated with crime have become a recognized part of our ever-growing vocabulary. In earlier centuries, *witch trial, horse thief, cattle rustler, frontier justice, vigilante, posse, slavenapper,* and *whipping post* were commonly used in newspaper headlines. Today cable news networks and Internet websites pepper "breaking

AMERICA'S OLDEST PRISON

Before the Battle of Baltimore, during the War of 1812, when Francis Scott Key wrote the "Star-Spangled Banner," it was there. While U.S. presidents John Adams and Thomas Jefferson were still alive, it was there. More than thirty years before Edgar Allan Poe wrote *The Raven*, it was there. Two decades before Samuel Clemens, better known as author Mark Twain, was born, it was there. And it still stands and functions today.

"It" is the Maryland Penitentiary, which opened in 1811 and whose original castlelike, Romanesque construction contrasts with Baltimore's nearby row-house neighborhoods, office buildings, and modern skyline. Originally built in a rural area the bustling port city had not yet reached, the institution has been labeled America's oldest operating prison. Some believe it is the oldest functioning penitentiary in the Western world. Admittedly, its current appearance is the result of untold additions, renovations, and demolitions, and its present-day staff is responsible for many more services, treatments, and functions than when the prison first opened its doors.

The walls of the two-centuries-old jail hold more than the state's newest crop of criminals. What remains of its dated architecture reflects a historical collage of society's ever-changing attempts to incarcerate, punish, and rehabilitate its offenders. From the day the first prisoner—convicted murderer "Negro Bob" Butler—was deloused, given his prison news" segments with such newer terms as *serial killer, carjacking, identity theft, white-collar crime, alleged suspect, person of interest, criminology, penology,* and *community policing.*

But certain aspects of crime never change. There will always be murders, manslaughters, robberies, embezzlements, rapes, disappearances, drug overdoses, suicides, and political scandals. These sensationalistic crimes grab headlines, and like an insatiable beast, cable news is always there, eager and willing to give the worst

clothing, and directed into a communal cell to serve his time, America's oldest operating lockup has generated tens of thousands of tales.

In *A Monument to Good Intentions: The Story of the Maryland Penitentiary, 1804–1995,* Wallace Shugg details the institution's origins and history. But the most interesting reading is the reports of escapes and beatings, tales of wardens and work gangs, stories of executions and public protests, and documentation of everyday suffering, riots, and death behind bars. Inside the imposing walls, convicts were beaten, whipped, and executed. Since 1924, all of Maryland's executions have taken place in the Baltimore prison, and the dead bodies of eighty-three prisoners, convicted of either murder or rape, were then carried out from the death chamber.

Having existed at the same location for nearly two centuries, the fifteen-acre penal complex periodically attracts the attention of students, reporters, and film crews. Andrew Stritch, a forty-year employee who has created a minimuseum of prison artifacts, is the prison's unofficial historian and tour guide. In addition to his regular duties in the complex's Maryland Transition Center, Stritch is considered the go-to person for history, facts, and stories about the penitentiary's colorful past.

The imposing stone structure presents the classic image of a "big house" as featured in black-and-white gangster movies. In 1979, scenes of star Al Pacino in front of the arched stone Maryland Penitentiary entrance were filmed for *And Justice for All,* a movie set in Baltimore that was later nominated for two Academy Awards.

evildoers round-the-clock coverage. Such was the case during a string of stunning murders in October 2002.

In that month, a series of random killings began in Maryland and spread to Virginia and Washington, D.C. For three weeks, the growing string of fatal crimes attracted the nation's attention and caused citizens in the affected jurisdictions to adjust their daily schedules. Schools were closed, police patrols were increased, and the press aired periodic live updates about the killer nicknamed the "Beltway Sniper," also called the "D.C. Sniper," "Washington Sniper," "Serial Sniper," and "Tarot Card Killer." When the two perpetrators were eventually captured, Maryland's reputation as a state that was reluctant to seek the death penalty played a role in prosecutors' deciding to put the alleged killers on trial first in the commonwealth of Virginia. That adjacent southern jurisdiction had a reputation for being much tougher on criminals, and it was not hesitant to seek and, more important, apply the death penalty.

Where crime is concerned, the old adage "Everything changes, except the calendar" is as true as the unknown day it was first uttered.

In the early 1800s, Dorchester County's Patty Cannon killed babies and unsuspecting travelers who sought overnight lodging in her home, burying their remains under her front porch. She also kidnapped slaves who had escaped into nearby Northern states and sold them back into slavery. During that era, such horrifying and "unladylike" deeds were rare. The evil woman accused of the crimes was considered a vile monster. But her despicable actions still fascinated a curious, entertainment-hungry public that lined up outside newspaper offices to purchase each edition of the local periodicals that detailed her horrific acts.

Unfortunately, during the last few decades, similar actions, or worse, occur so often that harried news viewers rarely take notice or pause from their daily routine. In Maryland alone, after a State Department diplomat's mind snapped, the Bethesda man bludgeoned his family members in their sleep and set their bodies afire in a pit; a twenty-year-old painter killed a Montgomery County doctor and his three daughters at the home where he was working; a Carroll County suburban homemaker was sucked into the strange new world of cyberspace adventures and ended up in a shallow grave; a Montgomery County husband had his family killed by an executioner who followed the steps outlined in a mail-order murder "how-to" manual; in Harford County, a convicted cop killer was released from prison and committed suicide after robbing a bank; and despite serious law enforcement efforts, in Baltimore the annual murder rate consistently approaches the three hundred mark.

Throughout the country, parents of schoolchildren worry about kidnappings, carjackings, and sexual predators entering their homes—not through locked doors or fastened windows, but by using the ever-growing, addictive, and intrusive powers of the Internet.

Today high-profile serial killers aren't unusual; they're simply new names added to an ever-growing list. Murderers, molesters, and kidnappers become instant celebrities—receiving publishing contracts, becoming the subjects of TV-movies, and having their images plastered on posters and T-shirts. There's even an Internet community that is eager to purchase a killer's possessions or the weapons used during heinous crimes, causing many to wonder how far our society has advanced—or regressed—in its acceptance of, and interest in, crime.

CHAPTER 2
Lovers' Lane Murders

* * *

The bells of the Glen Burnie Methodist Church tolled at 6:30 in the morning on a crisp September weekend in 1948. Within a short time, nearly one thousand searchers arrived. The volunteers would spend the entire day combing nearby forests and fields. Their objective: to locate any clues that might help determine the whereabouts of Mary C. Kline, age eighteen, a typist, and John H. Mahlan, twenty-five, a war veteran and postal employee.

The two town residents lived only a few blocks apart. They had been seeing each other for some time and had gone out on a date the previous Friday evening, but they never returned. On September 17, their bloodstained, bullet-marked car—containing no bodies—was discovered at the end of a side road, near a bean patch and hidden from passing view by a clump of trees. That area, near Old Annapolis Road and Lipin's Corner, was nothing like it is today. In the years following World War II, Glen Burnie was still a rural area, a grassy respite in contrast to the daily bustle of nearby big-city Baltimore.

The sleepy village had not yet been devoured by rampant development. Sixty years ago, there were numerous secluded spots near town where romantically inclined couples could park under the stars to talk and kiss. There still were "lovers' lanes."

Initial examination of the empty car by the police was beginning to indicate that the couple's romantic evening interlude had most likely proved deadly. Investigators said it appeared that a bullet had been fired through the passenger seat window. Shards of shattered glass were found on the right front seat. A bullet, flattened after apparently striking the steering wheel, was discovered in the car. A female's shoe, most likely Kline's, was resting on the floor of the backseat beside a pool of blood.

Police also reported finding Mahlan's driver's license in the woods, a little less than a mile from the car. But there was no trace of the bodies or even a hint of where they might be. It was hoped that the massive search, the second in two days, would help locate the two missing victims.

Unlike today, such a sensational crime was uncommon during the postwar years, and the Glen Burnie community was all but deserted during the hunt. The *Washington Post* reported that volunteers were transported to the search area by trucks and private cars. "Red Cross workers accompanied the searchers, supplying sandwiches and hot coffee as, hour on hour, men, women and children scoured the woodlands . . . Private planes and National Guard aircraft droned overhead. A bloodhound, property of a nearby resident, was also pressed into service."

Acting speedily, the Glen Burnie Improvement Association announced a $1,000 reward for information related to the case, but police cautioned patience. There wasn't much they could do until the missing persons, or their bodies, were found.

Within the week, police learned their investigation involved a double homicide. A county employee operating a road grader six miles west of Annapolis—about twenty-six miles south from where the victims' car was discovered—came upon the lifeless bodies of the missing couple. After an initial examination of the battered and bruised corpses, police theorized there had been a fight. Both victims had been shot in the head, but police did not locate a weapon. Apparently the murderer had dumped the bodies at the scene and then driven Mahlan's automobile back to Glen Burnie, where it had been found abandoned.

Police initially told the press that the killer may have planted clues to lead authorities to the small African American settlement of Freetown, in the vicinity of Pipins Corner, near where the car had been discovered. The results of the autopsy indicated that Mary Kline might have been held and terrorized for up to six hours after her male companion had been killed. Police followed a growing number of leads, including owners of bloodstained clothing, provided by area dry-cleaning establishments, as well as drifters and other suspects that might have been motivated by jealousy, vengeance, or robbery.

John E. Kline, father of the murdered young lady, said the killer was also a thief, telling reporters, "My girl's bracelet and watch were gone, and the boy's watch was gone." He believed that "someone who knew the neighborhood" had committed the crimes.

The twin murders continued to command the public's attention, as every development was reported in lengthy newspaper stories. Maryland governor William Preston Lane Jr. responded personally to appeals from the Kline family to look into the investigation. He visited the Glen Burnie police chief and later called on the Kline family at their home. The meeting took place soon after the Klines had returned from their daughter's funeral. The governor also visited the Mahlan home but learned that the family was in New York, where their son's funeral and burial were being held.

Police continued combing the sites where the bodies were found and the automobile had been abandoned. A week after the murder, they reported discovering six empty cartridges within two miles of the bullet-ridden car.

Medical examiners eventually determined that the young lady had not been raped in association with the murder. A bizarre twist involving her corpse occurred when seven young men were arrested for breaking into the Baltimore city morgue. Somehow the group entered the site where Mary Kline's body was stored and took pictures of the slain girl. They were charged with having taken obscene images of the girl's body. After thorough questioning, the police indicated that the men were not involved in the murder.

Becoming increasingly frustrated after nearly two weeks without a breakthrough in the case, the police followed every lead, thoroughly reviewing Mary's diary and interviewing a rejected suitor, several marines, gas station attendants, and locals from the surrounding area. On October 2, 1948, the *Washington Post* headline said it all: "Police Admit Hitting Stone Wall in Auto Slaying of 2: Girl's Diary Fails to Lead to Suspect, Anne Arundel Detectives Say."

Anne Arundel County Police Chief John H. Souers told reporters: "We have run down every clue and every lead—and have wound up without a single motive for the crime . . . We are still hopeful something might turn up to point to the killer." Despite nearly three weeks of questioning dozens of persons of interest, and receiving nearly fifty letters from locals and untold telephone tips, "all have been systematically investigated and found wanting," he acknowledged.

Soon after the article appeared, Chief Souers requested state assistance. In response, Governor Lane immediately established a "special squad of sleuths" to work all-out to solve the Glen Burnie double slayings.

Newspapers, providing details of the crime to a hungry public in an era before twenty-four-hour cable news, offered daily headlines indicating little significant progress: "7 More to Be Grilled in Auto Slayings" (October 9); "Arundel Probe Still Stalemated" (October 11); "Oyster Shucker to Be Grilled in Double Slaying" (October 13).

In an effort to salve the community's fear and frustration—and provide the impression that officials were serious about bringing the still-unidentified killer to justice—the Anne Arundel County grand jury announced it would meet with law enforcement personnel to learn directly about their efforts in the high-profile case. The *Washington Post* reported that Judge Benjamin Michaelson, in charge of the grand jury, proposed the meeting "because of criticism that has been directed at the law enforcement officials."

By November 1, Maryland police had followed leads and questioned possible suspects as far away as Boston and New Jersey. But the primary suspect was located a lot closer to home—in Freetown, about three miles southeast of Glen Burnie.

Residents sighed with relief, nearly two months following the slaying, when they read the November 11 headline: "Glen Burnie Slayer of 2 Caught, Say Md. Police: Laborer Charged with Murder; Gun of Foreign Make Checks with Shells."

Thomas Alexander Edwards, twenty-three, a three-year Army veteran who worked in a Baltimore sugar refinery, was in custody and charged with the crimes after he "fell into a trap baited by a stool pigeon."

The accused had been questioned three weeks earlier, when police learned that Edwards owned a strange, foreign-made handgun. After five days, Edwards, a former U.S. Army Quartermaster Corps soldier, was released after he said he had bought the weapon from a fellow soldier two years earlier, but had recently sold it to a "man he didn't know."

Police kept the suspect under surveillance, and he was picked up for an additional round of interrogation. While he was awaiting questioning, a former prison inmate in the adjoining cell was working as a police informant. In recorded conversations between the two men, Edwards's comments gave police enough reason to search his home. There they found the .380-caliber Czechoslovakian pistol, hidden behind a pile of fruit. After examination at the FBI laboratory, tests confirmed that the rare, foreign-manufactured weapon matched the bullets taken from the heads of the victims in the Lovers' Lane killings and found near the crime scene.

The high-profile case, which for two months had seemed to progress at a snail's pace, picked up speed as developments moved more rapidly following Edwards's arrest. The November 12 large-type *Washington Post* headline proclaimed: "Robbery His Motive: Suspect Admits Glen Burnie Murders, Lane Announces." In reporter Richard Morris's story in the *Post*, Edwards confessed he shot Mahlan through the car window as the young man sat in the driver's seat. When the female companion screamed and ran from the automobile, Edwards said he chased her down and forced her into the backseat, where he struck her in the head with the butt of his pistol. Thinking the girl also was dead, the killer drove the bodies to the "Sand Pit" outside Annapolis, where the bodies were later found by a county worker who alerted police.

The accused said he eventually kicked the bodies out of the car but heard the young woman moan. When she rolled over on the ground, Edwards admitted, he shot her in the head. Leaving the victims in the southern end of the county, he drove back to the Glen Burnie area, where he left the car in the woods and returned to his home in nearby Freetown.

Police described the confessed murderer as "arrogant and hard-boiled, a fast talker but a very shrewd and smart fellow, one of the toughest to crack." During the seventeen-hour interrogation, conducted over three days, he tried to direct blame toward one of his four brothers and several cousins, who he said all had access to the murder weapon. When picked up for questioning, Edwards's brothers offered conflicting stories about the weapon.

For several weeks, the police had endured a stretch of bad publicity, with the press suggesting investigators had been stymied and were running around in circles. Apparently eager to communicate the hard work and time devoted to the much-publicized case, the next day police released more details of their investigation.

Edwards had been under surveillance for several weeks before his arrest. As early as October 11, less than a month after the killings, police interrogated the accused, focusing on the location and possession of his rare-caliber weapon. At first he claimed he had sold the pistol to a man who had worked aboard a ship in Baltimore but could not remember the buyer's name. Despite conflicts in his gun story, police were not positive they had found their man and released the killer. But they placed him under constant observation.

When detectives saw Edwards return to the scene of the crime, they knew they had their man. Investigators trailing the suspect watched as Edwards searched the ground where he had first come upon the couple—outside Glen Burnie, only half a mile from his home—and fired the shot that killed the driver. Police believed the shooter was trying to locate the spent cartridge from the fatal bullet. They also had found casings twenty-six miles away, near Annapolis, where Mary Kline had been shot and the bodies dumped and later found.

After his second arrest, Edwards took authorities on a guided tour, reenacting his route the night of the murders and backing up his confession by offering additional details about how the murders had been carried out. Edwards claimed he became angry when the car driven by Mahlan almost ran him down as it passed him on the road. The accused said he caught up with the driver and got into an argument, during which time he shot the young man.

Although the police could not find two missing articles—Mary Kline's wristwatch and John Mahlan's wallet—Edwards denied to investigators that he had robbed the victims. But police still believed that they had found the killer and the case would be closed after a guilty verdict was achieved.

Surprisingly, in mid-December, a month following his arrest, and despite the cooperative and extremely detailed confession, Edwards pleaded "not guilty" to the Glen Burnie Lovers' Lane murders. A three-judge, nonjury trial was scheduled to begin hearing the case in early February, with fifty-two witnesses scheduled to testify for the prosecution and thirty-four for the defense.

The trial was held in Baltimore, away from the emotionally charged community in nearby Anne Arundel County, and lasted three days. Despite defense attempts to create the impression that Edwards's eleven-page confession was coerced and inaccurate, and that the state had planted evidence, the judges deliberated only an hour and found the accused guilty of first-degree murder.

The convicted killer's defense immediately requested that a new trial be presented before the judges of Baltimore's Supreme Bench. The attorneys suggested they would introduce evidence proving that the timing associated with the discovery of the shell casing matching Edwards's gun had "all the indications of a plant by authorities" designed to frame their client.

After hearing testimony, six of the seven Supreme Bench justices that considered the motion for retrial denied the appeal, and Edwards was sentenced to hang. The police and public closed the books on the Lovers' Lane case, thinking all legal proceedings were over. But six months later, in December 1949, an anonymous letter was discovered in the mailbox of Edwards's attorney, claiming the twice-convicted killer's innocence.

Gentlemen:

I am writing to you to let you both know that the Negro Edwards did not kill Mary Kline and Johnny Mahlan. The night that they were killed my budy [*sic*] had date with Mary Kline and I had one with another girl, both of them we met at the ice cream parlor in Glen Burnie. We were to meet them where Johnny and Mary Kline were killed. They were to be in a car driven by Mary's friend. When we got there Mary was with Johnny. A fight started. John slug [*sic*] my pal in the jaw. A pistol, a German Luger, was used on Johnny. Mary screamed. We both were scared. Mary was shot because she said that [she] was going to tell the police . . . Jack [the other man present] father says not to tell anyone because we both would be hanged . . . If you will promise me by writing a statement in one of the papers in Nashville, Tenn., that we will not be hanged or sent to prison for life, we both will come back to Baltimore. Are leaving Balto. for Christmas. You will find the pistol in the river under the bridge in Annapolis. Pray for us not the Negro.

It was signed with one word: "Tennesseans." But as the case was already closed, and the convicted killer sentenced, the police refused to follow up on this new piece of evidence.

In February 1950, Marylanders learned that the state's Court of Appeals—which threw out Edwards's original confession, as well as the convicted killer's comments to a prison stool pigeon and information he had provided during the tour of the killing sites—had granted the accused a new trial. As a result, the original lower court conviction by the three Baltimore judges was overturned. But the string of appeals associated with the case eventually came to a close, slightly more than two years following the murders. Edwards was finally convicted on December 12, 1950, and was sentenced to death.

In March 1952, however, Maryland's next governor, Theodore McKeldin, spared Edwards's life, commuting his death sentence to life imprisonment. The governor said he made his decision based on the controversy surrounding the case, because the verdict relied on circumstantial evidence and because of repeated charges that the police had failed to follow up on new evidence.

CHAPTER 3
The Smiling
"Assassinator"

* * *

The two most memorable moments in the political life of George Corley Wallace occurred nine years apart. The first event took place in Alabama, and all the parties involved planned it, particularly Wallace himself. The second incident happened in Maryland, but only one individual knew in advance what was going to happen—and it wasn't the controversial governor of Alabama.

In both instances, the events grabbed the national spotlight and put Wallace's picture on the front page of nearly every newspaper and magazine in the country. To his supporters in the South, the first instance marked one of the high points of his political career. The second, more tragic incident was viewed universally as the unexpected climax of Wallace's colorful life and the beginning of the end of his national influence.

In 1963, at his inauguration as governor of Alabama, the feisty orator vowed to a cheering crowd, "Segregation now! Segregation tomorrow! And segregation forever!" His words reflected the separatist sentiments of many of his state's electorate, and Wallace's remarks sent out a message to civil rights activists throughout the region that segregation was to remain a part of the heritage and lifestyle of America's Deep South.

Later that year, the U.S. Justice Department ordered the integration of the University of Alabama at its Tuscaloosa campus. On June 11, two African American students, Vivian Malone and James Hood, were escorted onto the campus to enroll in the upcoming summer session.

In response, Wallace announced he would make his "stand in the schoolhouse door" to oppose, symbolically, the forced admission of African Americans to the segregated school. He blocked the doorway to Foster Auditorium and said to a national audience watching the drama unfold on black-and-white television screens, "The unwelcome, unwanted, unwarranted and force-induced intrusion upon the campus of the University of Alabama today, of the might of the central government, offers a frightful example of oppression of the rights, privileges and sovereignty of this state by officers of the federal government."

Although the governor's grandstanding had no effect on the admission of black students to the campus, the short-statured, fiery speaker from Alabama who openly challenged Washington's federal bureaucrats became an instant folk hero to segregationists and advocates of states' rights. To those working to erase discrimination and end the country's separate-but-equal policies, however, Wallace was a villain who symbolized everything that was wrong with the South.

But love him or hate him, Wallace had leaped onto the national stage, and it was there he decided to stay.

In 1966, when Alabama's term limits barred Wallace from seeking another term as governor, his wife, Lurleen, ran for office in his stead, proclaiming openly she would "let George do it" if she were elected. When she won the election, her husband essentially ran the state government as a shadow governor, until his wife's death in 1968.

That year, Wallace cashed in on his name recognition and entered the presidential election—against Democrat Hubert Humphrey and Republican Richard Nixon—as a third-party candidate representing the American Independent Party. While offering a segregationist platform, Wallace used his considerable speech-making skills to paint himself as an outsider challenging established Washington insiders. He also attacked the Democratic Party's close association with longhaired and lawbreaking antiwar activists, who had rioted in Chicago and later threatened to disrupt Wallace's rallies and events.

In the 1968 November presidential election, this charismatic, Don Quixote–type figure won nearly 10 million votes, 13 percent of the popular vote, and carried five states—Arkansas, Louisiana, Mississippi, Alabama, and Georgia—with forty-six electoral votes. A few months earlier, as the campaign headed toward Election Day, some politicians had begun to worry that Wallace might attract enough support and electoral votes to steer the 1968 election process into the U.S. House of Representatives.

After winning another term as Alabama governor in 1970, Wallace made a second run for the White House. This time he entered as a candidate in the 1972 Democratic Party primary process, abandoning segregation and instead touting a law-and-order, states' rights, antiwelfare platform. At the age of fifty-two, the energetic candidate—who was accustomed to encountering hecklers at many of his stops—wore a bulletproof vest under his shirt and gave all of his speeches from behind an 800-pound bulletproof podium. Following the assassinations of John and Robert Kennedy and Martin Luther King Jr., Wallace acknowledged he was a tempting target, saying in a *Detroit Press* interview: "Somebody's going to get me one of these days. I can just see a little guy out there that nobody's paying any attention to. He reaches into his pocket and out comes the little gun, like that Sirhan guy that got Kennedy."

On May 15, 1972, Wallace was campaigning in Maryland. The border state had given the governor nearly 180,000 votes four years earlier, and the atmosphere among the crowd of about 1,000 in the Laurel Shopping Center was friendly and excited.

The few hecklers did not seem to pose a serious threat or cause Wallace and his bodyguards any concern. At the end of his law-and-order, vote-for-the-underdog speech, the candidate stepped from behind the bulletproof podium and began shaking hands with those in the crowd. It was hot and humid, so Wallace had decided before the event to leave off his bulletproof vest. Stepping down from the platform, he took off his suit jacket, rolled up his sleeves, and headed into the crowd. That's where a "little guy," dressed in patriotic red, white, and blue, was waiting. As Wallace had predicted, he was the kind of guy nobody was "paying any attention to"—until the gunshots went off.

* * *

Arthur Bremer was born on August 21, 1950, in Milwaukee. He was one of five children of Sylvia and William Bremer, whose household was the scene of drunken conflicts, loud arguments, and constant tension. Young Arthur created a fantasy world where he tried to escape from his surroundings. In a school assignment, he wrote that he pretended to be "living with a television family and there was no yelling at home and no one hit me."

The youngster developed into a shy, withdrawn student, who seemed intelligent but earned only mediocre grades. At school, Bremer had no friends and was ignored rather than taunted by his classmates. But as author Denise Noe noted in "The Attempted Assassination of George Wallace" on the website crimemagazine .com, Bremer's "expression began being distorted by the perpetual smile that would one day become infamous." According to Thomas Healy in *The Two Deaths of George Wallace*, Bremer's schoolmates "bestowed on him the hated nickname 'Clown.'"

In his diary, Bremer had described his thoughts during his days in school. "No English or History test was ever as hard, no math final exam ever as difficult as waiting in a school lunch line alone, waiting to eat alone . . . while hundreds huddled & gossiped & roared & laughed & stared at me."

As his early school years passed, Bremer never got into serious trouble, but he considered suicide and became withdrawn, eventually pulling back from interaction with his family. He began to exhibit the classic traits of a loner.

In 1971, Bremer worked as a busboy at the Milwaukee Athletic Club, but his habit of mumbling to himself while collecting dirty dishes from the diners' tables disturbed some of the patrons. Their complaints caused Bremer to be demoted to a position that kept him out of sight, working in the club's kitchen. Upset, he filed a discrimination complaint. The investigator who interviewed Bremer decided his complaint was unjustified and suggested to Bremer he was "bordering on paranoia" and should receive psychiatric attention.

Outraged at the findings, Bremer dismissed the suggestion and the investigator's efforts to arrange for professional help. He quit the job and moved on to another low-paying position, this time as a janitor at an elementary school, where he attempted to date a girl whom he had met at the school. Having had no experience interacting properly with women, his attempts at establishing a relationship were disastrous, and the girl described him as "goofy" and "weird."

Turning his attention to firearms, Bremer purchased two handguns. As in each of his previous new undertakings, failure exhibited itself early. During target practice at the gun club, Bremer shot holes in the ceiling instead of the target. Soon afterward, a police officer found him asleep in his car, parked in front of a synagogue, with bullets scattered across the front seat. He was arrested and fined for disorderly conduct.

Bremer's diary, which he began in March 1972, presents a picture of a depressed young man who was dogged by a series of experiences that resulted in others labeling him a loner and a failure. After reading about famous American assassins, Bremer decided he would claim his own famous place in American history by murdering a high-level politician. In his first entry, Bremer wrote, "Now I start my diary of my personal plot to kill by pistol either Richard Nixon or George Wallace."

Unlike most other presidential assassins in American history, Bremer's decision was not politically motivated. He was planning to shoot a major American figure so that his would become a household name. In his diary, Bremer stated his objective as "to do SOME-THING BOLD AND DRAMATIC, FORCEFUL & DYNAMIC, A STATEMENT of my manhood for the world to see."

Apparently, Bremer—who wrote he had decided to go by the term "assassinator," since he considered the word *assassin* "so ordinary"—had selected Richard Nixon. The president was a more prominent figure and therefore, Bremer decided, more worthy of his attention. His second choice, Wallace, on the other hand, would be more accessible. Placing himself on a level with John Wilkes Booth, Lincoln's killer, Bremer decided he must devise a catchy phrase to utter immediately after shooting his prey. "Got to think up something cute to shout out after I kill him [Nixon], like Booth did," he wrote.

Booth had shouted, "Sic semper tyrannis!" a Latin phrase meaning "Thus always to tyrants." When planning what he would say when asked why he had assassinated Nixon, Bremer wrote some of his options: "I don't know," "Nothing else to do," "Why not," or "I have to kill somebody."

To place his plan into motion, Bremer would fly to New York City. There he planned to rent a car; drive to Ottawa, Ontario, in Canada; and shoot the president, who was scheduled to appear there at a public event. On April 3, the day before he headed to the airport, Bremer wrapped his diary in aluminum foil and masking tape, placed it in a briefcase, and buried it in a landfill.

As had occurred his entire life, fate delivered another series of mishaps that plagued the aspiring killer in his attempt at gaining international fame. While in New York City, Bremer sought the services of a prostitute, but the experience was thwarted because he did not have enough money. He accidentally discharged his weapon in his hotel room, and when he hid his pistol in the wheel well of his rental car, it fell so far down that he was unable to pull it back out.

Upon reaching Ottawa, Bremer discovered that security was so tight he could not get close to his target, Richard Nixon. The "assassinator's" frustration was compounded by his belief that anti-Nixon demonstrators were attracting too much media attention while he was being overlooked. Writing later, in his second diary, Bremer indicated his annoyance with a photographer at one of the rallies: "What a dope! Those noisemakers were all on news film. He should of [*sic*] photographed the quiet ones. He never pointed his camera at me."

Upset that he had not been able to carry out his plans to kill Nixon, Bremer wrote that his second choice, George Wallace, would "have the honor" of being his victim. Thus the serious stalking of Alabama's colorful governor began.

Bremer started attending Wallace campaign events in Michigan and Maryland. He developed a new "cute phrase"—"A penny for your thoughts!"—which he intended to shout immediately following the murder. But the "assassinator" was still concerned that shooting his secondary target would not get him as much media attention and long-lasting recognition as killing the president of the United States.

In a Maryland suburb, not far from Washington, D.C., Wallace was scheduled to speak at a shopping center, the last stop before the Maryland and Michigan Democratic Party primary elections, both scheduled for the next day. According to a May 29, 1972, *Time* magazine article, Wallace said he was worried about Maryland, and the governor had told a friend, "Somebody's going to get killed before this primary is over, and I hope it's not me."

Being identified as a controversial politician on the national stage, Wallace was well aware of the dangers associated with his public profession and its extraordinary demands, which often placed him in harm's way. He had lived through the assassinations of the

Kennedy brothers and King. In a May 16 *Washington Post* article, Wallace spokesman Joseph Azbell recalled how the governor had commented about a possible attempt on his life: "Joe, there is always that threat that some nut is going to come along . . . I can't worry about what might happen. What I must worry about is winning this campaign."

And that quest for the Democratic nomination, with a long cross-country road to the White House, had brought Wallace into the border state of Maryland. During his statewide journey, Wallace had experienced interference at several previous events. Three weeks earlier, in Hagerstown in northern Maryland, young whites and blacks had disrupted his speech. A week later, while the candidate was leaving a rally in Frederick, someone threw a brick that hit him in the chest. At the University of Maryland, students threw Popsicles toward him.

In Wheaton, a week before the Laurel stop, protestors shouted "Hitler for vice president!" and tried to hit Wallace with tomatoes and eggs. When none reached their target, the candidate suggested to a thrower that a baseball team would be happy to see him as an opposing pitcher. Among the Wheaton audience stood a neatly dressed, blond young man, who was proudly sporting a large "Wallace" button and flashing a clownlike grin.

More than 1,000 spectators had gathered in front of the temporary stage erected in the parking lot of the Laurel Shopping Center late in the sunny afternoon of May 15, 1972. Up to fifty policemen patrolled the rally site, plus a number of Secret Service agents and the governor's private bodyguards. A country-western band, Billy Grammer and the Travel On Boys, had been onstage, warming up the crowd. When the strains of "Dixie" traveled among the excited audience, Wallace appeared, waving and smiling.

The governor launched into his standard stump speech, using several well-received lines that attacked "pointy-headed intellectuals who can't park their bicycles straight." Shouts from the back of the crowd urged the southerner to "go back to Alabama!" Wallace pressed on, speaking for nearly an hour as he attacked school busing and the *Washington Post*, as well as "social schemers" and "ultra-false liberals."

Referring to the country's leaders, Wallace shouted, "There's more pluperfect hypocrisy in Washington, D.C., and I mean politicians, than anywhere else in the United States." And the crowd responded with a rousing cheer. He urged his supporters to vote in the upcoming primary so that they would "shake the eyeteeth of the Democratic Party. Let's give 'em the St. Vitus dance. And tell 'em a vote for George Wallace is a vote for the average citizen."

Concluding his remarks to a long round of enthusiastic applause, Wallace smiled and left his protective podium. He began to work the crowd. Responding to an elderly woman wearing a "Wallace" hat, who shouted, "Over here, George! Over here!" the governor handed his coat to an aide and headed in her direction. Along the way, he pressed the flesh, grabbing hands and saying, "Nice to see ya!" to several clapping fans he passed in the supportive crowd.

✳ ✳ ✳

Among the throng of devoted followers and locals out to see a presidential candidate in their hometown stood Bremer. He had been following Wallace for weeks, waiting for his chance to make history. As the candidate moved closer, Bremer thrust out his arm in the midst of the mass of people. When his hand was less than two feet from his target, the twenty-one-year-old, unemployed ex-janitor pulled the trigger of his snub-nosed, .38-caliber revolver five times. The bullets hit Wallace, who fell bleeding onto the parking lot's black surface. Also wounded were Alabama State Police captain E. C. Dothard, who was hit in the stomach; Secret Service agent Nicholas Zarvos, who was shot in the throat; and Wallace campaign worker Dora Thompson, who received a bullet in her right leg.

The stunned crowd scattered, knocking into other bystanders and smashing into a table covered with Wallace campaign materials. In a *Washington Post* article describing the scene, a couple from Laurel said they had stood next to the assailant during the rally. They had been shaking the governor's hand when the shots went off.

"I thought he [the shooter] was for Governor Wallace," the wife said, "because when we would applaud, he would applaud. It just shocked me."

Wallace lay on the ground, blood streaming from his right arm and lower right ribs. He was taken to Holy Cross Hospital in Silver Spring, Maryland. Doctors discovered the presidential candidate had been struck five times, but the bullet that had hit his spinal canal delivered the most severe damage. Wallace had no feeling in his legs, and he would never walk again.

Throughout the attack and transport to the hospital, the feisty campaigner never lost consciousness, and he seemed to be more interested in consoling his second wife, Cornelia, who he had married only sixteen months earlier. Not surprisingly, the timing of Bremer's botched assassination attempt proved beneficial to Wallace in the two primaries held the next day. Democratic Party voters in both Michigan and Maryland gave Wallace two of the most impressive victories of his career. In Maryland, the wounded governor captured 39 percent of the vote. Hubert Humphrey followed with 27 percent, and George McGovern came in last with 22 percent. In Michigan, where forced busing was a hot-button issue, Wallace grabbed an astounding 51 percent of the vote, with 27 percent of the voters selecting McGovern, and an embarrassing 16 percent of those voting giving Humphrey last place.

As Wallace survived the attack, Bremer's unsuccessful assassination attempt continued his long losing streak of missteps that had plagued him since childhood. In the excitement that followed the shooting, with Bremer being wrestled to the ground amid crowd shouts of "Kill him!" he never delivered his "cute phrase"—the one he had hoped would help him claim a permanent place in the history books.

Following his capture and incarceration, Bremer was ordered to stand trial. Defense attempts to classify Bremer as mentally unbalanced were defeated by the prosecution, which pointed to the defendant's well-planned efforts to stalk and assassinate his human prey. Entries from Bremer's diary seemed to help the prosecution more than the defense. The trial started less than three months after Wallace was shot, and it lasted only one week. Bremer was sentenced to fifty-three years in Maryland's state prison system. This would be his last major failure, and it earned him nothing more than a slight historical footnote—and one that would become shorter over time.

But Bremer's conviction was not the end of the story. Many others—including Laurel residents, presidential candidates, Alabama politicians, occupants of the White House, and members of the law enforcement community—would be affected by the "assassinator's" actions.

* * *

Newspaper reporters and conspiracy theorists began investigating the shooter's background, as well as a number of somewhat curious events that reportedly had occurred immediately following the shooting. Many questions and unexplained circumstances persist to this day:

- Bremer fired five shots, but Wallace received up to five wounds, and three other people also were struck. Some suggest the large number of injuries indicates there may have been a second shooter.
- Bremer's fingerprints were not found on the gun recovered at the scene.
- A man was seen departing the Laurel parking lot immediately after the shooting, but a police bulletin originally issued for the unknown man's apprehension was soon canceled.
- Newspeople traveling with Wallace on the campaign trail had noticed Bremer on several occasions, but the unusual-looking man apparently had not attracted the attention of

trained security staff assigned to the candidate. And when in Canada, Bremer had even stayed in the same hotel as several dozen Secret Service agents.

- Where did Bremer—a former busboy and janitor—get his money to follow Nixon to Canada, stay in the Waldorf Astoria in New York City, purchase a car and weapons, and follow Wallace in Michigan and throughout Maryland? Tax forms found in the shooter's Milwaukee apartment indicated he had earned less than $2,000 annually.
- How was the FBI able to enter Bremer's apartment in Milwaukee less than forty-five minutes after the shootings, well before Bremer officially was identified as the shooter? There also are reports that the apartment was left unlocked and unguarded for nearly an hour, allowing anyone to place information at, or take materials from, the scene.
- Despite constant descriptions that Bremer was a loner, there are reports that he had met with a large man on a Great Lakes ferry in both April and May. Bremer also reportedly was seen in the company of demonstrators who were distributing anti-Wallace pamphlets in Michigan.
- Nixon ordered the FBI to take jurisdiction of the investigation away from the Secret Service.

These and additional unanswered questions and comments over the years have helped generate suggestions about possible government agency involvement in the Wallace shooting and a subsequent cover-up.

A series of White House tape recordings, released in 2002, indicates that when word of the shooting in Laurel reached the president, Nixon and his aides moved quickly into high spin mode. In a conversation in the Old Executive Office Building that afternoon, Nixon is heard suggesting that his staff release information to the press stating that Bremer was associated with the Democrats. "Just say he [Bremer] was a supporter of McGovern and [Ted] Kennedy,"

Nixon ordered. The president later added, "Just say you have it on unmistakable evidence."

Immediately following the shooting, Wallace announced that he intended to continue his pursuit of the Democratic Party nomination from his wheelchair, reminding supporters that Franklin Delano Roosevelt won World War II without the use of his legs. Wallace eventually dropped out of the national race, but he continued to serve as Alabama governor until his term ended in 1979. In 1982, Wallace again ran for governor, and he won that election. In 1987, he announced his retirement from public life. In the latter years of his political career, he modified his segregationist stance, apologized for his earlier antiblack views, and was recognized as a symbol of racial reconciliation. As a result, he received a significant number of African American votes in his later elections for governor of Alabama. Wallace died of respiratory failure and cardiac arrest on September 13, 1998.

Arthur Bremer never expressed remorse for his actions, and at one parole hearing, he argued for his early release by explaining that his attack on Wallace was not as serious as an attack on a "mainstream politician."

Bremer was released from the Maryland Correctional Institution in Hagerstown on November 9, 2007, after serving about two-thirds of his sentence. It was thirty-five years after the shooting. Bremer was paroled seventeen years ahead of his fifty-three-year sentence based on a system that rewards prisoners for good behavior. Throughout his confinement, the prisoner declined to give any interviews. It's reported that Bremer is living in Allegheny County, in northwestern Maryland. He is being monitored by parole officials and must wear an electronic monitor until his sentence is officially complete on June 15, 2025.

According to the *New York Times*, in December 1992, George Wallace Jr. requested that president-elect Bill Clinton reopen the investigations into the assassination attempt on his father. The Alabama governor's son's actions were based on a *New York Times Magazine* article reporting that then-president Richard Nixon and an aide had discussed planting Democratic opponent George McGovern's campaign literature in Bremer's apartment, but the plan had to be dropped because the FBI had gained control of the shooter's apartment so quickly. The younger Wallace also mentioned reports of Bremer meeting several times on a ferry in Michigan "with someone who worked directly for President Nixon" and said: "I do know that Bremer stalked my father for several weeks, staying in some of the finest hotels in the country. I have always wondered how a twenty-one-year-old man with no visible means of support could enjoy such a comfortable lifestyle."

While stating that he did not believe President Nixon had any prior knowledge of Bremer's intentions before the assassination attempt, the Alabama governor's son asked, "My question is: Did anyone else involved in Nixon's campaign have prior knowledge?" The late Alabama governor's former chief aide, Elvin Stanton, commented that George Wallace Sr. believed that top government officials were involved in a conspiracy in 1972 to eliminate him from the presidential race.

Those unsatisfied with official government reports on the Wallace assassination attempt, as well as incomplete answers to several conspiracy-related questions, point out that the shooting occurred in 1972, the same year as the Watergate break-in that led to Richard M. Nixon's resignation from office two years later. All of the personnel involved in what has become known as the "Dirty Tricks" era of Nixon's presidential campaign effort were operating from the White House during the Bremer shooting. Some believe that perhaps Alabama governor and Democratic presidential candidate George C. Wallace was another target of the infamous "Dirty Tricks" team.

In "Bremer & Wallace: It's Déjà Vu All Over Again," Lisa Pease investigated who would benefit from Wallace's removal from the 1972 presidential race. With the Vietnam War dividing the country, George McGovern, the Democratic Party's avowed antiwar candidate, was challenging former vice president Hubert Humphrey, a more moderate candidate. If Wallace had not won that major party's nomination, and then mounted another third-party run, as he had done in the past, it would have made the 1972 political campaign a three-way race. According to Pease, "McGovern could never have won in a direct fight with Nixon, as history proved. But with Wallace splitting the conservative vote, McGovern had a chance of becoming president. Clearly, those who supported the Vietnam engagement gained when Wallace was taken out of the running by the bullets in Laurel, Maryland."

No historical marker indicates the shopping-center location in Laurel where the shooting of George Wallace and three others occurred that spring afternoon in 1972. On the thirty-fifth anniversary of the shooting in May 2007, and with Arthur Bremer's early release from prison in November of that year, attention again turned to the site of the tragic and historic event. But reporters who visited the busy shopping center found that few passersby could identify the shooting site, and fewer still were aware that the assassination attempt had occurred there.

In an article titled "Bremer's Release Prompts Memories of Laurel's Worst Day," Dan Lamothe wrote: "Traces of the shooting can be hard to find. There is no marker at the shopping center, a complex near Route 1 that features about 50 stores, including a Giant Food supermarket, a CVS pharmacy and a Chuck E. Cheese restaurant. A Bank of America was built on the exact location Wallace, a fiery segregationist, was shot." And according to Ben Evans in "Memory of Gov. Wallace Shooting Fades": "No one seems to know what happened to the wooden stage that the shopping center would roll out for community events and that Wallace stood upon to deliver his stump speech before wading into the crowd. The bank that sits alone in the middle of the parking lot—and is closest to the shooting site—once displayed a large photograph of the scene in the lobby. But the national chain that bought the bank took it down years ago."

Perhaps, the site might have more historical and tourist value, warranting a marker of some kind, if Wallace had not held such unacceptable segregationist views and if Bremer had accomplished his mission. Summarizing the thoughts of local merchants and a Laurel city spokesperson during interviews in May 2007, Evans wrote: "Memorials are more common at sites where historical figures died, such as John F. Kennedy in Dallas or the Rev. Martin Luther King Jr. in Memphis. There is no marker, for example, at the Washington hotel where President Reagan was wounded in a 1981 shooting."

CHAPTER 4

Searching for a Bishop and a Sign from "The Lord"

* * *

Disappearances have never failed to attract the public's attention, especially when the missing person is a high-profile personality or the circumstances surrounding the sudden absence are linked to a sensational crime.

On November 24, 1971, a man in sunglasses, using the name Dan or D. B. Cooper, hijacked a Northwest Orient airliner and, during the night, parachuted out above the Cascade Mountains in the northwest wilderness near the border of Oregon and Washington. The hijacker had a ransom of $200,000 in cash strapped to his body, and he hasn't been seen since.

On July 30, 1975, former Teamsters Union president James R. "Jimmy" Hoffa disappeared from the parking lot of the Machus Red Fox restaurant in West Bloomfield, Michigan, near Detroit. Despite

45

rumors he is buried under the 50-yard line of Giants Stadium in East Rutherford, New Jersey, the location of Hoffa's body has never been found. The fiery union leader was declared dead in 1983.

In the state of Maryland, the whereabouts of a gambling figure and an alleged murderer remain of interest in their respective jurisdictions' cold-case files, and police are as eager to apprehend these two suspects as they were more than three decades ago, when the men were last seen. As the years have passed, both individuals have achieved legendary status, and whenever clues regarding their whereabouts surface, their stories generate new headlines and stimulate the imagination of still-curious readers.

Diplomat on the Run

Near Washington, D.C., on March 1, 1976, William Bradford Bishop Jr. told his secretary at his U.S. State Department office he was feeling ill, probably coming down with the flu. The career federal bureaucrat worked as an assistant chief in the Special Trade Activities and Commercial Treaties Division, Office of International Trade, Bureau of Economic and Business Affairs. He left work early and returned to his home in Bethesda, Maryland.

That was the last day he was ever seen at work, or by any of his neighbors and friends in the upscale Carderock Springs neighborhood. It's also the last day anyone saw any of the other five Bishop family members alive.

For the next week, the split-level home was silent. Bishop's sixty-eight-year-old mother, Lobelia, who lived in the house, didn't take her daily walk with the family dog, Leo. None of the three children—William Bradford III, fourteen; Brenton Germaine, ten; and Geoffrey Cordon, five—played in the yard or rushed in and out the home's kitchen door. Nor did the diplomat's wife, Annette, thirty-seven, drive to the grocery store or work in her garden. Bishop didn't show up at work the rest of that week, either. But no one in the State Department office called the Bishop home, not wanting to disturb him, since they believed he was home ill, recovering from the flu.

It wasn't until March 8, a week after he had left work unexpect-edly, that a concerned neighbor who had noticed the lack of activ-ity in the Bishop family home contacted Montgomery County police. Officers responded to the curious neighbor's call by visiting the house on Lilly Stone Drive and entering through the unlocked front door. Inside the foyer, they noticed traces of blood. A search of the premises revealed the presence of blood splattered in several bedrooms and across the home's walls and carpets. They also found remnants of bloodstains in the driveway. But no bodies, nor the fam-ily dog, were located during the initial search of the property.

As the investigation progressed, police discovered that after leaving work on March 1, Bishop had withdrawn $400 from his bank account. He had also stopped at a Sears store in the Mont-gomery Mall, where he bought a mallet-style hammer and a two-and-a-half-gallon gasoline can.

But the pieces of the puzzling investigation actually had begun to fall into place a week earlier, when the North Carolina State Bureau of Investigation broadcast a report throughout the East Coast of five dead bodies that were found in the woods of Tyrrell County. The rural region of 400 square miles of swamp, forest, and cropland was iso-lated, with only about 800 residents.

According to the *Washington Post*, Forest Ranger Ronald Brick-house was patrolling the North Carolina swampland on March 2, a day after Bishop had left his Washington, D.C., office. Brickhouse received a radio call from another ranger, who reported a brush fire about six miles south of Columbia, North Carolina. Brickhouse rushed immediately to the site and began fighting the blaze. After about ten minutes, the surprised ranger said, "I saw two bodies in a hole."

Afraid that the killer might still be in the area, Brickhouse left the scene and used his two-way radio to alert authorities. When the sher-iff arrived, he and his men cleared the area and pulled five bodies from a shallow open grave. The pit holding the smoldering corpses of two women and three children was about forty feet off a logging road and half a mile from the nearest house. It was described as a "bathtub-sized grave," about three feet deep, six feet long, and four feet wide. A gasoline can, long-handled shovel, garden fork, and tire tracks also were found near the scene.

North Carolina police traced the shovel's serial number and label to a hardware store in Potomac, Maryland. When the Montgomery County police discovered the bloodstains in the Bishop home on March 8, they recalled the earlier bulletin they had received about the five burned bodies in North Carolina, with the Maryland hardware store connection. At that time, the Maryland and North Carolina investigations began to come together to help solve the two states' related murder puzzles.

Police constructed a scenario in which Bishop probably first beat his wife, Annette, to death with the hammer, and then used the weapon on the rest of the family. Based on the location and amounts of blood found, they believed the children were killed while sleeping in their beds. That night, Bishop apparently dragged the bodies into his 1974 Chevrolet station wagon and, with his golden retriever, drove nearly 300 miles south to the North Carolina forest. The journey took about five hours. Using the tools he had purchased only the day before, Bishop dug a shallow hole, shoved the five bodies into the pit, doused the battered and bloodied remains with gasoline, and set his murdered family afire.

On March 18, more than two weeks after the bodies were found, Bishop's abandoned car was located at the other end of North Carolina, about 400 miles away, in Great Smoky Mountains National Park near the Tennessee border. Inside the bloodstained car, authorities discovered blankets, probably used to cover the bodies during the initial trip south, plus an ax and a shotgun.

Experts believe Bishop's attention to detail and planning of the alleged multiple murders enabled the suspected killer to take advantage of a two-week head start and put a fair amount of distance between himself and the law.

In a 2006 article in Raleigh's *News & Observer*, marking the thirtieth anniversary of the discovery of the Bishop murder victims, reporter Jerry Allegood wrote: "Five corpses would create a stir in any community, but the gruesome find was particularly unsettling in Columbia, a town of about 900 about 170 miles east of Raleigh. The whole county, a sparsely populated area known for farming and fishing, hadn't had a slaying in about 40 years."

Brickhouse, since retired from the state forest service, was the first person to discover the burning bodies, which he initially thought was a pile of discarded hogs. "When you walk up expecting to see hogs and you find people, boy your belly goes," he told reporters during an interview in March 1976.

But the question remains: Whatever happened to Bradford Bishop Jr.? There are plenty of possibilities:

- He could have died in the forest after being burned by flames from the pit.
- He may have fallen victim to an accident as he tried to escape through the woods.
- He may have committed suicide.
- An accomplice might have been waiting to help him get away.
- He could have been mauled or killed by wild animals, such as the region's black bears, as he made his escape on foot.
- He could have defected to Russia.
- He may have slipped out of the country and be living abroad.

Based on Bishop's intelligence background, the last scenario may be the most likely.

Bishop was thirty-nine at the time of his disappearance. He was a Yale University graduate and former army intelligence officer, trained in counterintelligence. As a midlevel diplomat with the State Department, he had served in U.S. embassies in Italy, Ethiopia, and Botswana and was fluent in five languages: English, Spanish, French, Italian, and Serbo-Croatian.

A *Time* magazine article on March 22, 1976, reported that neither Bishop's neighbors nor his relatives recalled any marital problems between Bishop and his wife. But some friends thought Bishop might have resented his domineering mother, who lived with the family. "Still others," the article said, "suspected that Bishop might have been a spy and that he and his family could be victims of a rubout reminiscent of the film *Three Days of the Condor*. But no persuasive proof was offered to support this theory."

Interviews with relatives and neighbors did not suggest the presence of any apparent marital problems in the Bishop household, nor were there any hints of stress created by family or financial pressures. The couple had been together since their high school sweetheart days in Southern California. To all appearances, they were the storybook, all-American couple: Bradford, the confident football quarterback, and Annette, the popular, attractive cheerleader. After graduation, they were separated during their college years, with Bradford heading to the East Coast to earn his degree at Yale University. Annette studied closer to home and graduated from Cal-Berkeley.

To other residents of their comfortable, middle-class neighborhood, the Bishops' marital relationship and interaction with other families with children seemed absolutely normal. The couple enjoyed tennis, playing in a mixed doubles league at the neighborhood club. The Bishops often took friends of their children along on their family camping and skiing getaways. With no clear motive for the killings, officials surmised that after experiencing continual success in all his endeavors, the ambitious diplomat might have become depressed when he was passed over for a promotion at the State Department and essentially snapped.

The skills and training Bishop had used throughout his military and diplomatic careers may have enabled him to escape from the United States and start a new life in any number of foreign countries, some in which he had lived before. It also was suggested that Bishop may have been a spy for the U.S. State Department or the CIA, but both agencies denied this was the case.

A year after the killings, the *Baltimore Sun* reported: "The FBI has circulated Mr. Bishop's photograph and description throughout the world. It has placed stops with immigration authorities, credit agencies, Mr. Bishop's banks, airports, car rental agencies and any other type of business or service he could be expected to approach, including physicians, pharmacists and psychiatrists."

If Bishop had made plans to flee the country, his intelligence contacts would have made it relatively easy for him to obtain a number of false passports, which would be essential in such an escape. Disappearing and starting a new life with false documents was much easier to accomplish in 1976 than it is today, especially in the aftermath of 9/11.

Over the years, Bishop's story and authorities' efforts to locate the alleged murderer have been featured in a number of newspaper and magazine articles and on several popular, nationally aired television programs, including *Unsolved Mysteries*, an ABC *20/20* special called "Vanished," and *America's Most Wanted*. In a 1999 *Reader's Digest* article titled "World's Most Wanted," Bishop was one of the eight men whose stories were featured and read by millions around the world.

Sightings of Bishop have been reported in Belgium, Spain, Italy, Sweden, Germany, the Netherlands, Africa, Greece, England, Finland, Belgium, Russia, and Switzerland. According to a *Washington Post* story by Donald Baker, a family friend of the missing killer, who had worked with him when he was stationed in Ethiopia, reported to Swedish police that she saw Bishop twice in Stockholm during the summer of 1978. The FBI sent an agent to that city to follow up on the report and aid in the investigation, but apparently nothing concrete developed.

A year later, an employee of the Agency for International Development—who had worked with Bishop in the U.S. Embassy in Ethiopia in 1966 and at the U.S. State Department from 1974 until his disappearance in 1976—told Italian authorities and the FBI of an encounter with Bishop in Sorrento, Italy. In another *Washington*

Post story by Baker, the man reported that he had glanced at another man who was standing beside him in a men's room in the Italian resort city. Surprised at seeing someone he thought he knew, the U.S. citizen stared at the other man and asked if he were Brad Bishop. Immediately, the second man appeared startled and replied excitedly in English, "Oh, God, no!" and ran from the room. The man raced outside to follow the stranger, who looked very much like his former coworker Bishop, but he had fled and disappeared in a rainstorm. Bishop's former colleague also recalled an earlier conversation between the two men. It had occurred in February 1976, outside the State Department, when Bishop was very depressed after being passed over for a promotion. The fellow employee said he told Bishop, "There's always next year," to which his dejected colleague replied, "Yeah, if there is a next year."

The *Reader's Digest* article described a possible encounter in 1994, as a woman from Bethesda, Maryland, was waiting for her train to arrive in Basel, Switzerland. While standing on the platform, the woman gazed at a train at the other end of the station. Suddenly she noticed a well-groomed man open a window of his car and she immediately experienced the shock of recognition, But before she could tell anyone that the face she saw belonged to her former neighbor—and fugitive with an arrest warrant for five murders— the man she believed might be Bradford Bishop disappeared as his train pulled out of the station.

In a March 2006 *Washington Post* article titled "Where is Bradford Bishop?: 30 Years Later, Md. Murder Suspect's Flight Still a Puzzle," Paul Duggan reported that although there had been hundreds of reported sightings over the years, only three were by people who had known the fugitive. And these, Duggan wrote, "led authorities straight to dead ends."

An unexpected development occurred in 1992. Investigators who were reviewing the unsolved multiple-murder case uncovered a letter that had been sent by registered mail to Bishop's State Department office only two weeks after the 1976 killings and the diplomat's disappearance. According to an article by Associated Press writer Jonathan Moore, the correspondence had been sitting in a file, unread, for seventeen years. The letter was from the late A. Ken Bankston, an inmate at a federal prison in Illinois. The contents suggest that Bankston may have been involved in helping Bishop locate an assassin, who would kill the diplomat's family in exchange for a passport Bishop would provide as payment. The letter names two other convicts and also references a woman in a North Carolina correctional institution who was familiar with Phelps Lake and Creswell, two locations near the forest where the Bishop family bodies were discovered.

Although an analysis of the letter provided nothing that helped locate Bishop, its contents indicated that the frustrated diplomat had been making definite plans to murder his family. He also may have been arranging to meet up with a female accomplice in North Carolina, who would help him escape from the remote wooded area.

Bankston had died in 1983, and the letter wasn't discovered in Bishop's closed work files until 1992, so more than fifteen years had passed before police became aware of the unusual connection between the two men. Some wonder if Bishop may have been located and captured had the correspondence been found during the initial investigation immediately following the murders.

In an October 2006 article in the *Baltimore Sun* titled "After 30 Years, Bishop Killings Still a Mystery," reporter Fred Rasmussen interviewed Montgomery County Sheriff Raymond M. Kight, who was a county deputy at the time of the five murders in 1976. The sheriff, who has never forgotten the case, recalled staking out the Bishop house in the event the alleged murderer returned to the crime scene. Kight said he assumes Bishop is still alive, and his department follows every lead and continues to distribute age-enhancement posters. Chief Deputy Darren Popkin, who has been working on the Bishop case over the last fifteen years, has followed up on hundreds of leads. The investigation into Bishop's where-abouts has been a global search, and Popkin and Kight have traveled to several locations in the United States, including Minnesota and Texas, to work with federal and local law enforcement personnel on the Bishop case. "The Sheriff's Office," Popkin said, "will continue to follow up on every lead until Bishop is brought to justice and tried in court on this horrific crime."

The Bishop investigation, which *Washington Post* reporters Paul Duggan and Michael E. Ruane described as "one of the most enduring mysteries in the annals of local crime"—and which occurred while Gerald R. Ford was president—is still open.

Note: Anyone with information regarding William Bradford Bishop or his whereabouts should call the Montgomery County Sheriff's Office at 240-777-7022, contact a local Interpol office or police department, or email sheriff.fugitive@montgomerycounty md.gov.

Gambling Kingpin in the Wind

Many of those for whom gambling is a recreational diversion today are unaware that before state-operated lotteries, scratch-off tickets, Internet gaming, and slot machines at racetracks, gambling was conducted only in the shadows. A few decades ago, police were well aware of each city's "bookmakers," businessmen who solicited and catered to fortune seekers that eagerly bet on sports games, horse races, and daily numbers.

Essentially, state governments now offer legal games of chance, which had formerly been provided primarily by members of the Mob or independent neighborhood contractors called "bookies." The state decided it could control games of chance and grab its piece of the action, essentially cutting out the local, free-enterprise businessmen. Now government agencies oversee gambling, which generates much-needed revenue that continually fills the state treasury. It's really all semantics. Instead of the Mob emptying gamblers' pockets through independently run, illegal "gambling," the state tax office grabs money from approved recreational "gaming"—a more acceptable and less sinful-sounding term.

Back in the day, most bookmakers also operated legal businesses, which served as respectable fronts through which they funneled their illegal gambling earnings. In his article "Baltimore Gamblers: Betting by the Book," *Washington Post* writer William Gildea described most bookies as neighborhood shopkeepers who owned saloons, barbershops, groceries, and gas stations. Other bookmakers accepted bets as they frequented neighborhood social clubs, where they also set up shop. These shadowy merchants of chance were located on every block in larger American cities, including Baltimore. Gildea estimated that until about 1970, illegal bets on horses alone totaled tens of millions of dollars a year in the city.

A bookmaker's primary objective was to keep a low profile and avoid attracting the public's attention. One necessary expense, however, was paying off police and government officials to look the other way as the neighborhood gambling czar provided his age-old public service.

But there is always an exception.

Julius "The Lord" Salsbury was one of Baltimore's more colorful entrepreneurs and bookmakers. He attracted considerable public attention during his arrests, trials, convictions, and eventual disappearance. An October 2006 article by columnist Frederick N. Rasmussen in the *Baltimore Sun* indicated that longtime Charm City residents are still fascinated with the well-known gambler's story—even though nearly forty years have passed since "The Lord" last strolled Baltimore's streets.

In his column, Rasmussen noted that Salsbury—a former gambling figure and owner of a nightclub in Baltimore's adult strip-club district known as "The Block"—walked away from his northwest Baltimore home in the summer of 1970. The businessman had been convicted of a federal gambling charge and was out on the street awaiting an appeal, hoping to avoid a fifteen-year federal prison term. Salsbury, described by federal officials as Baltimore's "kingpin of gambling," directed his "empire" from an office in the basement of the Oasis Nite Club, located at Frederick and Baltimore Streets, not far from today's Inner Harbor.

Julius Salsbury's life on the edge began in the carefree years following World War II, when the young man learned the gambling trade from a few established figures in the business. In the late 1940s and early 1950s, Salsbury was arrested several times on bookmaking charges. During the subsequent years, he was picked up for operating a disorderly house in "The Block" and for failing to register as a gambler and purchase a federal betting stamp. A tax evasion conviction in 1963 resulted in a one-year stint in Allenwood Federal Prison, and federal tax liens amounting to nearly three-quarters of a million dollars—for failing to pay gambling, income, payroll, cabaret, and withholding taxes—made eye-catching headlines and good reading.

Salsbury's name and picture continued to appear periodically in regional news stories, solidifying his reputation as a local celebrity with a somewhat checkered past. Following a 1968 raid on the gambling kingpin's Oasis Club office, where tens of thousands of dollars in cash was confiscated, the Maryland U.S. attorney said the accused's operation was associated with an "elaborate underworld" that conducted millions of dollars in illegal business operations nationwide.

Despite a U.S. Supreme Court decision that overturned the gambling law that had been used as the basis for the 1968 raid and subsequent conviction, federal agents kept after Salsbury. He was too big a target and too colorful a character to take out of their sights. More importantly, the government had to justify its previous efforts by slapping Salsbury with a charge that would stick. Later that year, federal agents arrested him for interstate transfer of gambling checks. In 1969, he was convicted of collecting on sports betting across state lines. When his appeal was denied, and knowing he would eventually be sent to jail for more than a decade, the Baltimore bookmaker apparently made a difficult decision that would affect his life and those of his loved ones and friends.

Salsbury's wife, Susan, in a 1971 interview in the *Sun* magazine, remembered the last time she saw her husband, on August 13, 1970. She said the thought of serving fifteen years in prison weighed heavily on his mind. "When you see your husband going down the walk for the last time," she told the reporter, recalling her husband's exit from their home that summer night, "it's heartbreaking. That was it."

In April 1994, *Sun* reporter Michael Olesker made reference to the passing of Susan Salsbury. The reporter believed that law enforcement people would attend her funeral, in the event that her long-missing husband, who would have been seventy-eight years old at that time, might appear to witness the services.

"What happened to Julius Salsbury 36 years ago," one Baltimore police officer told the *Baltimore Sun* in 2006, "continues to be one of the great mysteries of our town."

According to Gildea, Salsbury dodged the law for many years, and then vanished without a trace. Some believe he escaped through Canada to a foreign country, possibly Israel or Cuba. But one colorful legend persists, suggesting "The Lord" exited the city, quite appropriately, in a horse trailer.

Olesker wrote that several of Salsbury's close associates secured the horse van, hid the gambler on the bottom, and drove him north, not letting him out until the escape vehicle had crossed the U.S. border into Canada. He added that those few people who might know "The Lord's" whereabouts are not talking. But some speculate he died in exile, coincidentally, only a few days before his wife.

Well-known movie producer and Baltimore native Barry Levinson, Gildea noted, seems to have used Salsbury as the model for Nate, the principal character in the 1999 movie *Liberty Heights*— named after a northwest Baltimore neighborhood. In the film, the bookmaker is a sympathetic figure that operates a strip club on "The Block," and leads a normal family life, but is arrested and eventually separated from his family.

Interestingly, in his article, "Gambling, Guns and These Changing Crimes," Olesker pointed out how notorious and threatening

Salsbury was considered just a few decades ago. But in actuality, he was a solitary businessman fulfilling a need that the government has since taken over and now offers as a legitimate product. Many law enforcement personnel considered Salsbury "a bad guy for gambling," Olesker wrote, "and newspapers put his name in front-page headlines. And today, a time of rampant murder and narcotics that ruin neighborhoods, we run three-paragraph stories of major police raids because they're no longer considered a very big deal."

Salsbury's friends and competitors described him as a generous and gracious businessman; he had no bodyguard, never carried a weapon, and was considerate of his associates and customers. Salsbury was placed on Interpol's "most wanted" international fugitives list in 1974. Today he would no doubt be far down the "most wanted" list—behind a large and growing number of murderers, serial killers, terrorists, child molesters, and white-collar criminals who think nothing of stealing billions from their investors' retirement accounts.

Note: Anyone with information regarding Julius Salsbury should call the City of Baltimore Cold Case Unit at 410-396-2121.

CHAPTER 5
Cop Killer

* * *

After tragic shootings in 1978 sent two police officers to their graves, to the shock and disgust of many, the killer escaped the state executioner and was sentenced to a lengthy stint in jail. But fate sometimes works in mysterious and surprising ways, as it did in 1997, when a single bullet to the head ended the convicted cop killer's life. Many interpreted this as delayed justice, and more than a few citizens found the event particularly satisfying, especially since the execution was administered by the killer's own hand.

The life and death of Terrence Johnson is about more than a series of criminal acts. It is a controversial saga involving racial strife, community mistrust, liberal activists, frustrated peace officers, spirited demonstrations, opportunistic intruders, judicial procedures, correctional practices, individual failure, and redemption. The story also includes the shock, pain, and frustration suffered by both the perpetrator's and victims' families and friends. Although the events generated intense public reactions spanning two decades, the story began very quietly, when two brothers decided to take a ride in Prince George's County late on a summer night.

About 2 A.M. on June 26, 1978, Terrence, age fifteen, and his older brother, Melvin, eighteen, were pulled over by police and arrested under suspicion of breaking into coin-operated laundry machines. The two officers, Albert M. "Rusty" Claggett IV, twenty-six, and James Brian Swart, twenty-five, transported the brothers to the Hyattsville police station for fingerprinting and questioning.

What occurred next depends on who's telling the story, but there was no doubt regarding the results of a scuffle that took place in the police station basement. Both Claggett and Swart were shot to death, and Terrence Johnson was subdued by other police officers—with Claggett's pistol, the murder weapon, clutched in the youth's hands.

In a community with a high percentage of African American residents and a very low percentage of black officers on the county police force in the mid-1970s, tensions between the two groups had been strained for some time. The deadly shootings and alleged beatings in the Hyattsville police station added to the sense of distrust and resulted in an emotional blaze that immediately flared out of control.

According to police sources, while the suspect was being fingerprinted in the basement of the building, Terrence Johnson began fighting with Claggett, grabbed the officer's weapon from its holster, and shot him. The prisoner immediately raced into the hall and fired five more shots, killing Swart, who received deadly bullet wounds in the stomach and back.

What seemed like an open-and-shut case that would send the killer to death row—particularly with several credible witnesses present at the scene of the killings—immediately took a dramatic 180-degree turn.

At Johnson's bond hearing two days later, the prosecuting state attorney referred to the prisoner as "a cold, calculating killer," while the defense attorney said he was "an average 15-year-old child." Judge Louis DiTrani said the shocking crime snuffed out the lives of "two men who were supposed to protect us from ourselves" and set bond at $1 million—representing $500,000 for each slain officer. The prosecutor had argued that if Johnson were released, he would leave the area. The defense and family members contended that the youngster must have been scared and/or provoked to take such desperate measures against his captors. The older brother, Melvin Johnson, who had been in a cell during the shootings, was held under $2,500 bond and charged as a rogue and vagabond.

Within the week, a nine-mile-long funeral procession entered the Gate of Heaven Cemetery in nearby Silver Spring, where the bodies of the two slain lawmen were buried. Grieving family members and hundreds of brother officers representing many jurisdictions mourned the fallen policemen, whose bodies rested in flag-draped coffins.

Meanwhile, friends of the Johnson family began to mobilize support for Terrence, primarily through individuals, churches, and organizations in the black community. Members of the Prince George's NAACP helped establish a defense fund. By August, Johnson's lawyers and those associated with civic and church groups and political action committees—including the Southern Christian Leadership Conference, Black United Front, Prisoner's Rights Coalition, Committee Church of Christ, and Concerned Clergy of Prince George's County—were actively seeking contributions. Fund-raising events were held, at which "Free Terrence Johnson" T-shirts were offered for sale, and in September, a "Free Terrence Johnson" rally was planned at the detention center.

One of the main issues was whether the defendant would be tried as a juvenile or an adult. According to a *Washington Post* article, in October, more than two hundred persons crowded the Prince George's County courthouse, where attendees heard Judge Vincent Femia denounce organized attempts by Johnson supporters to influence the court in the controversial murder case. Femia, who would decide whether the accused would be tried as a juvenile or an adult, announced his annoyance with the protest groups' efforts to pressure the court into handling the case in a different fashion because the defendant was black. "To suggest in this day and age," said Femia, "that justice should be determined on the basis of race is a gross insult to justice and a personal affront." He added that the content of the letters of support for Johnson he had received indicated that the writers "showed a total and complete ignorance of judicial sense." He told the overflow crowd, "You people don't know what we do here."

Femia presented the five criteria he would use to make his decision: age, mental and physical condition, amenability to treatment in the juvenile system, the nature of the offense, and the safety of the public. "All the walking, talking, foot-stomping and demonstrating won't do any good with this member of the bench," he said. "We're just going to play it by the book."

Despite testimony from a number of character witnesses called by the defense, the next day Femia announced that Johnson would stand trial as an adult for the two murder charges. The ruling meant that if convicted, Johnson could face life imprisonment. Had he been tried and convicted as a juvenile, he would have been released from custody at the age of twenty-one, after serving only six years.

By October, Johnson's supporters had raised enough money to post the $100,000 bond (10 percent of the original bail amount), and the accused killer was released from custody and sent to live with friends. But news articles and statements by law enforcement representatives and black community activists kept the controversial case in front of the public during the months leading up to the opening of the trial.

This March 1979 *Washington Post* headline summarized the dilemma that would face the decision makers at the trial: "Jury Hears Two Versions of Officers' Slayings." During opening statements, the defense said the jury would learn the story of a youngster frightened out of his mind and acting in self-defense. Terrence Johnson had been abused and threatened by Officer Swart at the time of the arrest, he claimed, and in the basement room of the police station, the accused was being beaten by Officer Claggett.

In contrast, the prosecutor advised the jury that it would be introduced to "an arrogant, explosive defendant, a person unlike the defendant sitting in this room," and that no sounds of an argument had come from the fingerprinting room, where the defendant shot and killed the first of two police officers.

The defense said that Terrence was kicked three times by Officer Swart, and two other officers took the boy in a corner and gave him a beating. He claimed that Officer Claggett threatened to break Johnson's neck. The lawyer described the physical struggle with Claggett as a fight for Johnson's life—an obvious effort to explain the accused's fragile state of mind and subsequent desperate actions.

When Johnson took the stand five days later, he testified his belief that Officer Claggett "was going to kill me," and said that the policeman had grabbed him and placed him in a headlock around his neck. It was during this scuffle that Johnson said he grabbed the gun and it went off. When he saw spots of red on Officer Claggett's clothing, he panicked.

Melvin Johnson testified that his younger brother ran out of the room and fired two shots but did not shoot Officer Swart. Other witnesses to the shooting in the hall contradicted the older brother's story, however.

To the surprise of law enforcement officers and the victims' families, on April 1, the jury of eight whites and four blacks—after deliberating more than eighteen hours over three days—acquitted Johnson of the two murder charges. But they found the now-sixteen-year-old defendant guilty of two lesser offenses—manslaughter and illegal use of a handgun—in the death of Officer Claggett, and not guilty by reason of insanity in the death of Officer Swart.

The opposing sides reacted immediately to what was called a "compromise verdict." Members of the slain policemen's families sobbed, and some officers voiced their disgust with the jury's decisions. Robert Johnson, father of the accused, told the *Washington Post*: "I guess in a way it's a relief. It could have been worse. But Terry still has to go to jail and that's terrible. In a way, I guess we were sort of lucky."

Prosecutor Arthur A. Marshall Jr. expressed his concern about how the verdict would affect the community. He told reporters it was apparent the jury believed there was "some kind of conspiracy in the police department, that the police department should be on trial."

In the end, the jury believed the argument that Johnson was a terrified youth, fearing for his life, as opposed to an arrogant, cold-blooded murderer.

In the days immediately following the verdict, newspapers and television reports focused on various aspects of the case and the verdict's effect on different groups of citizens throughout the community. In an opinion piece published in the *Washington Post* on April 2, Lawrence J. Hogan, county executive, urged both sides in the controversy to remain calm and work together for the good of the county. Hundreds of officers from the 837-member county police force ignored the official's plea and participated in an unauthorized "sick out," to demonstrate their intense disagreement with the results of the trial and their frustration with members of the public who were antagonistic toward the police. As one officer told the *Post*, "When we look around now in the community, it seems like no one cares about us."

A month later, rival groups, each numbering about one hundred demonstrators, gathered outside the county courthouse awaiting Johnson's sentencing decision. Activists' chants of "Free Terrence Johnson!" were countered by demands of "We want justice, 25 years!" The latter group, made up of police supporters, got its wish, letting out a loud cheer when they received word that the maximum sentence had been imposed. In response, Johnson's supporters began shouting: "We'll free him, we know it! We've got the power to show it!"

Despite the conclusion of the trial and sentencing, the lingering effects of the Terrence Johnson case were felt in Prince George's County for some time. Follow-up stories—on the convicted killer's status, his complaints about treatment while in custody, and denial of his appeal—appeared in newspapers. Each time, the articles revived heated emotions and painful memories many thought would be best left forgotten.

But no one could have imagined that nearly two decades later the now released Terrence Johnson, who, his supporters and members of the state parole board believed, had been successfully rehabilitated, would resurrect interest in the controversial closed 1978 murder case. He did so by claiming front-page headlines for his leading role in another crime, which occurred on his thirty-fourth birthday.

At 9:40 A.M. on February 27, 1997, Terrence Johnson and another brother, thirty-five-year-old Darryl, entered the NationsBank branch in Aberdeen, located in Beards Hill Shopping Center not far from I-95. Terrence carried a knife, and Darryl waved a gun. They demanded money and showed tellers and customers a box, which they said held a bomb. During the holdup, Darryl pressed a gun to one woman's cheek, saying if anyone moved or the cops came, he would blow everyone's brains out.

A few minutes later, the brothers raced from the bank, carrying $20,000 in cash. Police spotted the two suspects moving on foot, about a quarter mile from the crime scene. When officers got within fifteen feet of the suspects, they shouted instructions to both men, ordering them to lie on the ground. Darryl Johnson followed the order; Terrence did not.

Instead, the convicted cop killer, who had taken possession of his brother's gun after the robbery, pulled out the weapon, raised the barrel to his temple, and pulled the trigger. There would be no robbery trial for the paroled criminal—who, despite police objections, had been granted an early release from prison in 1995. The "model prisoner" had served only sixteen years of his twenty-five-year sentence for his 1978 crimes. As had occurred following his earlier arrest, members of the black community immediately offered support, sympathetic comments, and laments over the shocking end of Terrence Johnson's life.

According to an article in *The Capital* by Theresa Winslow, immediately following the shooting, Charles Ware, Johnson's lawyer, told Washington, D.C.'s, WTTG-TV that he did not believe Terrence had killed himself. The attorney claimed that police had shot the alleged bank robber and convicted cop killer, adding that he had a witness to prove his allegation. An Aberdeen police spokesman called the lawyer's comments "baseless and without merit," and Maryland's medical examiner later confirmed that the deadly wound to Johnson's head was self-inflicted. Soon afterward, Ware backed off his initial allegation and concurred with the coroner's finding.

Because of Terrence Johnson's earlier conviction, articles about the Aberdeen robbery referenced his role in the 1978 cop killings and informed readers about his experience in prison, early parole, adjustments to life on the outside, and ultimate return to his criminal ways.

Johnson appears to have been given every opportunity to better himself before and after he walked out of his state prison cell in 1995. While in Patuxent Institution, he earned an associate's degree from Baltimore Community College and a business degree in 1986 from a program for prisoners associated with Morgan State University. While in the Jessup Pre-Release Unit in 1989, he married a longtime girlfriend. In 1991, he was turned down for parole for the fourth time. But Johnson appealed the ruling, and with the help and recommendations of supporters, the killer's parole was finally approved, and he was released from prison in February 1995.

A well-intentioned couple gave Johnson free accommodations in their home. Members of a church he joined raised $10,000 for him to attend law school, and he found work as a paralegal. In the fall of 1995, he entered the University of District of Columbia law school. Howard University had refused his application after alumni and faculty voiced their strong opposition to his presence on that campus. To some elements of society, Johnson the ex-con was a local celebrity, and he made periodic appearances on radio and television talk shows. He and his lawyer also were exploring book and movie contracts about his fascinating life and experiences.

With so many positive developments and the high potential for a sparkling future, two obvious questions remained unanswered: Why had Johnson returned to crime, and why did he take his own life?

In a *Washington Times* article, Barrington Salmon and Sean Scully offered details about Johnson's activities during his second chance at life. Apparently, much of the well-intentioned assistance he received may have backfired. Instead of helping the ex-convict make the transition into society, gifts and support may actually have contributed to his decision to rob the bank and self-inflict his subsequent death. The paroled killer was experiencing financial difficulties and was in the process of being served with a paternity suit. He had to leave law school because funding for the scholarship he was expecting had been withdrawn. The people who had given him free rent returned to their home and asked him to leave.

One classmate described Johnson's life immediately after leaving prison as being firmly planted in the fast lane—visiting nightclubs, dining at nice restaurants, and attending sporting events. When he left prison, he immediately bought a $25,000 Toyota Celica convertible, but by 1997, he was behind in his payments, and the finance company was threatening to repossess his car. Johnson's attorney, Ware, told the *Washington Post*: "His reach often exceeded his grasp. He liked his lifestyle, and he liked parties and women, and he spent a lot of money . . . I used to call it 'accelerated living.'"

Others speculated that Johnson could not live up to the life his family and supporters expected of him. Those who had defended him for decades considered his educational achievements and return to society a glowing example of the success of rehabilitation. Johnson was going to be the first convicted criminal to earn a law degree and practice in the state of Maryland.

On March 4, a week after his suicide, nearly eight hundred mourners crammed into First Baptist Church of North Brentwood to pray and offer support for the young man who in 1978 had killed two policemen and in 1997 taken his own life. Clergy, family, classmates, and friends described Johnson as a victim of the system, whose life ended in tragedy, who succumbed to society's pressures, who could not adjust quickly enough to life on the outside. Words of kindness and disappointment were expressed during the public remembrance of his life, as were anger and frustration. One official of the National Black Police Association could not contain his anger, asking: "When are they going to make amends for what they did to him? He spent 17 years in prison and was turned loose."

But to many others, Johnson would always be a cold, calculating killer who had worked the system to his advantage, and they predicted, hoped, and waited for him to fall. These people did not pause to celebrate Johnson's life. Instead, they reflected on the significance of his death—and, to them, the more important loss of two young policemen whose killings were overlooked by Johnson's supporters. Those holding a less flattering opinion of the cop killer did not blame the system, but believed the criminal had brought his life experiences on himself. *USA Today* reported that friends of the families of the officers Johnson had killed considered the two-decades-old debt now paid in full. "Thank God justice has been done," said Officer Claggett's mother upon hearing the news of the robbery and Johnson's suicide. "I figured that he would get himself in trouble again, but I never really thought that it would be anything like this."

A day after the robbery, a hand-lettered sign appeared near an Aberdeen home, across the street from where Johnson had shot himself. It read: "A criminal is a criminal is a criminal, no matter how many books they write."

In October, eight months after the robbery, Johnson's brother Darryl was sentenced to twenty years in prison for his role in the Aberdeen bank holdup. According to the *Washington Post*, Johnson family members said Terrence had been living beyond his means and had run up massive credit card debt, apparently contributing to his decision to rob the bank. They also described Darryl as a "weaker sibling, dragged into the bank robbery by his strong-willed and better-known brother, Terrence."

Even after his death, Terrence Johnson remained a polarizing figure. In 1999, Kathy Gambrell of the Associated Press wrote, "The case sparked early discussions about whether juveniles should be charged as adults, whether people convicted of killing police officers should be granted early release and whether inmates can be rehabilitated."

CHAPTER 6

"Adios" and No Regrets

* * *

On May 17, 1994, John F. Thanos became the first prisoner to be executed in the state of Maryland in more than three decades. The convicted killer had spent a vast majority of his forty-three years in state institutions, committing additional crimes each time he was released. Thanos's sordid life story has been used as both an endorsement for swift application of the death penalty and a disappointing example of the ineffectiveness of the state's correctional system.

Thanos grew up in Dundalk, a working-class Baltimore-area neighborhood, peopled mainly by union households and families whose parents made their living in factories and at the nearby steel mill. The youngster's schooling in the 1950s and 1960s included periods of time in reform schools and mental treatment facilities.

In a courtroom session years later, an expert defense witness would suggest that Thanos's abusive family situation—in which an alcoholic father beat his wife and terrorized his only son—was a primary reason for the young man's antisocial behavior and deadly criminal career. It is an often used defense theory that "outside influences play an important contributing role in a criminal's actions," and in Thanos's case, this "dysfunctional family" argument may indeed have considerable merit. But a costly mistake by a prison official resulted in the crime-prone young man's release from the state's correctional system before he was eligible. This overlooked clerical error contributed to the deaths of three teenagers who otherwise would probably still be alive today if the killer had remained in jail where he belonged.

While growing up, Thanos was involved in minor altercations that caught the attention of school officials and earned him a reputation as a bully and a troublemaker. By the time he was eighteen, he had moved his criminal career up a notch, being admitted to an adult prison in Hagerstown for car theft and assault. He was paroled in 1968, but a year later, he committed and was convicted of his first known major crime, the rape of a woman in a motel in Baltimore County. He eventually served seventeen years of that twenty-one-year sentence, but it was not long before he was back in state custody.

In the September 28, 1990, *Baltimore Evening Sun*, Marina Sarris summarized Thanos's life of crime. The convicted rapist had "earned enough 'good time' credits to get out of prison in 1986, even though he later told psychiatrists he had attempted suicide in prison and was stabbed by another inmate," Sarris wrote. "Within a month of this release, he was back in jail on charges that he robbed a 7-Eleven convenience store." The reporter also uncovered a somewhat strange and perhaps prophetic bit of information: The Thanos family name resembles the Greek word *Thanatos*, which means "death personified." That turned out to be a rather accurate description of the troubled and violent young man.

By the age of thirty-five, Thanos had been in adult prison more than half his life and spent several years in juvenile facilities. He had been examined by mental health professionals and was identified as a drug and alcohol abuser, with "anti-social personality disorders" and a personality exhibiting "paranoid features."

To average citizens, law enforcement personnel, and most members of the legal and criminal justice communities, the public would have been best served if Thanos were kept behind bars. In April 1990, Thanos's address was a jail cell in Maryland's Eastern Correctional Facility in Somerset County, part of a rural area of the state known as the Eastern Shore. He was serving a seven-year sentence for the robbery he had committed less than a month following his previous "good time credits" release in 1986.

But Thanos never came close to paying his full prison-time debt to society. A miscalculation of good behavior credits released Thanos from prison on April 6, 1990—543 days early. No one would have been aware of the paperwork error, if only the career criminal had changed his ways. Unfortunately, that was not the case.

Less than five months later, on August 29, Thanos kidnapped and robbed a Salisbury cabdriver of $55 at gunpoint, and locked the victim in the trunk of his cab.

Two days after that, Thanos escalated his crimes to a deadly level. While hitchhiking in a rural area of Worcester County, on the southern Eastern Shore, Thanos was offered a ride by eighteen-year-old Gregory Taylor. Thanos produced a sawed-off shotgun from his duffel bag and directed the well-intentioned driver to head into a wooded area. That's where Thanos shot the young man three times in the head. Then the murderer headed north.

Three days later, on Labor Day, September 3, Thanos stopped at a Big Red gas station in Middle River, in Baltimore County slightly east of Baltimore. He demanded money from the clerk, sixteen-year-old Billy Winebrenner, who handed over the cash without resistance. As the teenager pleaded for his life, Thanos cold-bloodedly shot the young man in the head, and then turned the gun on fourteen-year-old Melody Pistorio, Billy's girlfriend, killing her as well.

In her *Baltimore Evening Sun* article, Sarris wrote: "Thanos, who has spent the bulk of his 41 years in reform schools and prisons, stands accused in a recent weeklong spree of robbery, kidnapping and gunfire. The spree ended with Thanos' capture on Sept. 4 after gunfights with Salisbury and Delaware police."

In January 1992—responding to a request by Thanos's three public defenders, citing possible adverse effects of pretrial publicity—the case involving the murders of Billy Winebrenner and Melody Pistorio had been moved to Oakland, in the western end of the state. During the proceedings, jurors and the public learned much more about Thanos and his distorted and frightening criminal mind.

CHARM CITY'S KILLING STREETS

Baltimore is one of the country's most historic cities. Tourists visit the home and gravesite of literary giant Edgar Allan Poe and attractions throughout the picturesque Inner Harbor. Camden Yards and Ravens Stadium draw tens of thousands of sports fans. And schoolchildren and historians as well as foreign visitors and politicians travel to Fort McHenry, this country's only National Monument and Historic Shrine, home of the "Star-Spangled Banner."

But Charm City residents and workers know that if visitors happen to stray a few blocks off the main thoroughfares in certain parts of city, they could be risking their lives. Take a few wrong turns, and strangers find the city's polished tourist avenues can turn quickly into Baltimore's mean and very deadly streets.

Each year, newspaper articles and television segments feature murder statistics of the country's largest cities, using the numbers as a gauge to determine the safest and most dangerous places in America. Consistently, Baltimore has been named one of the deadliest places to live, with more than 250 murders annually over the past decade. City officials blame

In her opening statement, state prosecutor Sue A. Schenning told the jury of seven men and five women that the evidence in the double murder trial they were about to hear was both horrifying and shocking. The state's goal was to show that the defendant's level of evil was so intense that he deserved nothing short of the death penalty.

Attorney James McCarthy, one of the accused killer's public defenders, referred to Thanos's videotaped confession and acknowledged "John Thanos did what he is charged." Essentially, the defense team's strategy was to secure a verdict that would spare Thanos a date with the executioner. Their best hope was to persuade the jury to place him back in prison, or in a mental institution, for the rest of his life, without any chance of parole or another "good behavior" early release.

the high number of killings on drug- and gang-related violence. This unflattering image of Baltimore has been reinforced over the last few years by the award-winning HBO series *The Wire*, set in the city's ghettos and drug-infested neighborhoods.

More than a decade ago, television viewers had already gotten a good look at Baltimore's seedy side through the highly acclaimed television series *Homicide: Life on the Streets*, which ran from 1993 to 1999. The show was produced by Baltimore native Barry Levinson, with a significant portion of the content based on the successful book *Homicide: A Year on the Killing Streets*, by David Simon. The author spent a year accompanying officers and detectives in Baltimore's Homicide Division. The television series was headquartered in Fells Point and filmed throughout the city, and many of the episodes were pulled from actual events.

The killing streak seems to continue, year after year, as an examination of the city's deadly criminal activity from 2005 to 2007 shows. In 2005, Baltimore experienced 269 murders, an average of five each week. The longest period without a killing was seven days. January saw thirty-three deaths linked to homicides—more than one each day. In "Murder by Numbers:

(continued on page 74)

A Look behind the Sad Statistics of Baltimore's 2005 Homicide Toll," *Baltimore City Paper* reporter Anna Ditkoff addressed the tragic effects of Charm City's consistently high killing rate, such as the frustration of law enforcement and judicial authorities to reduce the frequency of the crime and the devastating ripples of fear and grief that accompany each murder. To help the people left behind after a homicide, the State's Attorney's Office established the Family Bereavement Center to provide counseling and other services.

The next year, the count was even higher, at 276 murders. After analyzing the toll of killings for 2006, Forbes.com named Baltimore "the country's second most murderous city," following only Detroit.

At the end of 2007, WJZ-TV presented a summary of that year's deadly statistics. Jessica Kartalija noted that in January alone, on average, one

The jury selection took four days. The first-degree murder trial lasted only one day. The jury deliberations were much shorter—only thirty-five minutes.

That's how long it took to convict the defendant on all charges: two counts of first-degree murder, two counts of robbery with a dangerous weapon, and one count of using a handgun in the commission of a felony. The only question remaining was how Thanos would pay for his crimes. The same twelve jurors that had convicted the killer were about to hear—and see—a lot more of the defendant when they reconvened to sit through additional testimony that would decide Thanos's fate.

The prosecutor requested that the jury watch the killer's twenty-eight-minute taped confession a second time, so the members could see how he appeared calm and bored, yawning several times during the interrogation, showing no remorse.

The defense said it planned to introduce evidence to illustrate Thanos's "pain" and explain why the troubled youth had turned out the way he did.

person was murdered in Baltimore every twenty-nine hours. City police blamed the high number of killings on gun and gang violence and said Charm City's murder rate was out of control. Baltimore's 280 murders in 2007 affected every age group, including children, with 27 of the victims being under age eighteen. Associated Press writer Ben Nuckols noted that with a census population recorded at 631,366 for that year, Baltimore remained one of "the nation's worst cities for murder per capita, with about 44 slayings per 100,000 residents."

After the close of 2008, however, law enforcement personnel celebrated the results of their intensified efforts to thwart killings. The city's homicide total was reduced to 234, the lowest annual number in two decades. Only time will tell if the decline in murders continues, or if "Bodymore, Murdaland" reverses course and lives up to its unflattering nickname.

While the prosecutor described Thanos as vicious, vile, and evil, the defendant interrupted her, growling, "You're evil!" Despite orders from the judge to remain silent, Thanos continued to interrupt the prosecutor, snarling, "You're evil!" several times.

As the sentencing portion of the trial progressed, the prosecutor described Thanos as a "menace to society" and a "danger in every setting he's ever been in," saying that while his acts were sick and horrible, "he knew full well what he was doing. He knew it was against the law."

To bolster the defense argument, Thanos's attorney drew on the expertise of a certified social worker, who said she had interviewed Thanos's mother, aunt, and two sisters for more than twenty-one hours. She told the jury how Thanos's father had beaten, pushed, and kicked the young boy. At times, the elder Thanos would play "bogeyman," turning off all the lights and using a bright flashlight to search throughout the house for the young boy, terrorizing him in the process. Incidents of humiliation and mental cruelty were commonplace. According to one of Thanos's sisters, their father would drug his wife with sleeping pills and rape his daughter in the bed-room she shared with John Thanos.

During cross-examination, the prosecutor got the expert for the defense to admit that she had been told Thanos had tried to drown one of his sisters and had cut the head off her pet duck. But this information, the expert admitted, had not been included in her tes-timony as a witness for the defense.

If the jury had not been convinced that convicted killer John Thanos was as evil as the prosecution had contended at the very start of the trial, all doubts were swept aside during the defendant's vengeful and hate-filled performance on the witness stand.

The *Washington Post* headline certainly was an attention-grab-ber: "Killer of Md. Teens Says He Wants to Defile Corpses." And in the accompanying Associated Press story, the defendant's own words displayed the dark nature and extreme intensity of his evil personality. At the sentencing hearing, Thanos said he "would find pleasure in defiling the remains of the two teenage victims to tor-ment their grieving loved ones." He stated: "Their cries bring laugh-ter from the darkest caverns of my soul. I don't believe I could satisfy my thirst yet in this matter unless I was to be able to dig these brats' bones up out of their graves right now and beat them into powder and urinate on them and then stir it into a mercury yellow-ish elixir and serve it up to those loved ones."

During his fifteen-minute speech, Thanos taunted members of the youths' families who were present, calling them cowards for not avenging the deaths of their relatives by trying to kill him them-selves. He also made obscene gestures to prosecutors and threat-ened his own attorneys and their family members. He claimed to cast a spell of cancer on the female organs of prosecutor Schenning, calling her a "hysterical woman." At the conclusion of the sentenc-ing hearing, Thanos was sentenced to death in the gas chamber for his crimes.

But while a stream of publicity surrounded Thanos's sensational trial and conviction for the two 1990 Labor Day murders outside

Baltimore, the killer would ultimately be executed for the shooting death three days earlier of Gregory Taylor in rural Worcester County. In April 1993, the Maryland Court of Appeals had upheld Thanos's conviction and death sentence in the Taylor case.

In nearly every case involving application of the death penalty, a lengthy series of appeals drags the execution process out for decades, causing the convicted killer an extended stay on death row and delaying closure for the family members of the victim. Possibly one of the few good things Thanos did in his sordid life was adamantly denying his attorneys' efforts—and those of ACLU representatives and family members who attempted to lobby on his behalf—to appeal his impending death sentence.

Therefore, on May 17, 1994, Thanos moved ahead of thirteen other inmates waiting a date to enter Maryland's death chamber, where he would be put to death by lethal injection. When asked if he had any final words, the career criminal and killer replied, "Adios," and waited silently for the drugs that would put him to sleep and stop his heart to take effect.

Afterward, there were more editorials condemning the state's legal execution than there were columns supporting the action, although a WBAL-TV poll found "broad support" for executing the murderer—89 percent in favor, with only 8 percent wanting the court to consider appeals by the killer's family. Groups of protestors against capital punishment and supporters of Thanos's legal execution showed up outside the Maryland Penitentiary in downtown Baltimore, where the sentence had been carried out. One woman held a worn and tattered sign proclaiming: "Eye for Eye. He Should Die."

In a *Baltimore Sun* story, "Thanos Died Quietly after a Life of Fury," Michael Ollove and Sandy Banisky reported that Maryland Governor Donald Schaefer had been asleep at the time of the 1 A.M. execution and did not learn of Thanos's death until he arose in the morning. "Later, he [the governor] had no compassion for the dead killer. 'This isn't a memorial, you know,' Mr. Schaefer said. 'This isn't some hero's death. This is the death of a man who had committed an atrocious crime. I didn't look upon it as a day that we're going to lower the flag. When I found out he had no mercy,' the governor said, 'I have no feeling for Thanos at all.'"

Numerous experts in criminal justice, law, and medicine analyzed the potential effects of the execution in the days leading up to, and immediately following, the rare application of Maryland's death penalty law. But it was the relatives of the victims that provided the most valuable insight. In a *Washington Times* article by Kristan Metzler, family members mentioned their satisfaction that the state had carried out what they believed to be the appropriate form of justice, allowing a final sense of closure to begin. In a statement to reporters in the early-morning hours following the execution, Joanie Pistorio—who, along with her husband, Ed, had been denied permission to witness the execution of their daughter's killer—questioned whether punishment by lethal injection matched the severity of Thanos's horrific crimes. "It's too easy," she said. "You don't shoot three children in the head and go to sleep to be put to death. Don't we all wish our death will come that easy?"

CHAPTER 7
Hit Man Murders

* * *

A triple murder in a Maryland suburb during the winter of 1993 set in motion one of the lengthiest and most far-reaching police investigations in Montgomery County history. By the time the killers were apprehended, the long arm of the law had solved a complex puzzle whose pieces had been scattered in Detroit, Hollywood, and Boulder, Colorado.

The crime occurred sometime early in the morning on Wednesday, March 3, 1993. At 7:30 A.M., as she did each day, Vivian Rice approached the home of Mildred Elizabeth Horn, forty-three, who lived in the Silver Spring house with her disabled son, eight-year-old Trevor. The early-morning visit wasn't unusual. Rice, a relative who lived nearby, routinely checked on the family each morning. Before entering, she noticed that a light had been left burning in the empty garage and the family's new Chevrolet Astro van was missing.

Sensing something was wrong, Rice left and returned with a neighbor. Together they entered the home and were shocked to find two dead bodies lying in the foyer. Both women—Mildred Horn and

Janice Saunders, thirty-eight, the overnight nurse who cared for the disabled young boy—had been shot at close range in the eyes. Horn's body had three bullet wounds, and Saunders's had two. Rice ran from the scene screaming, and the neighbor called the police. Authorities arrived and soon determined that the killer also had suffocated the quadriplegic boy by removing his respirator tube. The alarm bell connected to the youngster's emergency generator was still blaring when police entered the crime scene.

The two other Horn children were not at home on the night of the killings. Nineteen-year-old Tiffani, a student at Howard University, was at school, and Tamielle, Trevor's twin, had slept overnight at her aunt and grandmother's house, which was nearby.

Police estimated that the three murders had occurred between 2 A.M., when the nurse made her last entry in Trevor's logbook, and 5:30 A.M., when a newspaper carrier recalled seeing the light burning in the empty garage. The killer apparently had accessed the home by breaking and crawling through a narrow basement window.

Mildred Horn had worked as an American Airlines flight attendant for twenty years. She was scheduled to be on an 8:07 A.M. flight to San Juan, Puerto Rico, leaving from Baltimore-Washington International Airport. Coworkers later said they were surprised and concerned when the dependable employee did not show up on time for work. By the afternoon of the murders, police found the missing van in a nearby parking lot. They theorized that the killer had parked his car at the site, walked to the Horn home, and used the murdered family's van to make his escape from the crime scene.

At the request of Maryland investigators, Los Angeles police questioned Mildred's ex-husband, Lawrence Horn, fifty-three, at his Hollywood home for several hours on Wednesday afternoon. The independent record producer and sound engineer, who had once held a significant position with Motown Records, said he was unaware of the slayings. The Horns had been married in Las Vegas in 1973, but within a few years, their relationship soured. The twins were born in 1984. In 1987, the parents were divorced and became involved in a custody dispute. Lawrence was behind in child support payments, had moved from the area, and in subsequent years, had little contact with his children.

What caught the attention of police and the victims' relatives was the significant amount of money Lawrence Horn was suddenly in a position to inherit because of the sudden deaths of his family members. The estate was estimated at between $1 million and $2 million. This was primarily the result of a 1990 settlement of a malpractice lawsuit the Horn family had filed against Children's Hospital National Medical Center. In 1984, the Horn twins were born three months premature, with underdeveloped lungs. At eleven months old, Trevor suffered severe brain damage while being treated at the hospital.

A week after the killings, the *Washington Post* reported that Lawrence Horn acknowledged Montgomery County authorities still considered him a suspect. Police, however, did not provide any details about the investigation, other than saying Trevor's estate might have been a "prime motive" in the case. Attorneys specializing in estate law commented that according to Maryland law, Lawrence Horn, as Trevor's surviving parent, would probably inherit the young victim's estate, including the $1.1 million the disabled youngster was to receive when he turned eighteen.

More than five hundred friends of the Horn family attended an emotional funeral service, held at Mount Calvary Baptist Church in Rockville, honoring the slain mother and son. Relatives expressed sorrow and demanded that the killer be brought to justice. Lawrence Horn was absent from the ceremony. "Horn said police advised him not to attend last Saturday's funeral for Mildred and Trevor," reported the *Post* article, "because 'they could not ensure my safety' in light of the 'amount of animosity' toward him from Mildred Horn's family. 'The [family] considers me to be the most likely person to have done it, and they cannot accept that I had nothing to do with it,' Horn said, adding that he plans to come to Montgomery County this week with his mother and other relatives to hold a memorial service at Trevor's grave."

Lawrence Horn's life had gone from the mean streets of Detroit to the glam and glitter of Hollywood. It led him back to a small, run-down California apartment, from which he hoped to reclaim some of his lost fame and glory. In December 1962, a friend hired Horn, then a twenty-two-year-old sound technician, for $50 a week to work in a converted garage, the unassuming headquarters for a fledgling business named Motown Records. Horn proved that being in the right place at the right time could have astonishing results. Within a few short years, he was mixing recordings by day and mixing it up at night with the likes of Smokey Robinson, Gladys Knight, the Four Tops, Diana Ross, and Stevie Wonder. According to Kevin Sullivan of the *Washington Post*, unlimited expense accounts, overnights at five-star hotels, rides in chauffeured limos, and hanging out with the rich and famous were everyday experiences for the poor baker's son from Detroit's west side.

Thirty-two years later, in the summer of 1994, Horn was running with a much lower class of associates. As a result of this dramatic career decline, and his apparent decision to supplement his dwindling income through a deadly crime, the ex-husband and father of the Maryland murder victims—along with his partner, James Edward Perry, forty-five, from Detroit—was indicted by a Montgomery County grand jury on three counts of murder and one count of conspiracy. The down-on-his-luck freelance producer and his alleged hit-man partner were arrested by federal agents in Hollywood and Detroit and escorted back to Maryland for trial.

According to the *Baltimore Sun*, Montgomery County police called their work on the case "the most exhaustive and labor-intensive" investigation in the department's history, during which detectives logged more than 3,000 hours. The Montgomery County state's attorney described the murders as being "planned long in advance and arranged with a great deal of preparation and evil."

In October 1995, James Perry was brought to trial. The accused killer referred to himself as a "case-buster," someone on the street who could get things done. Perry's business card read: "The House of Wisdom, Dr. J. Perry, Cold Reader, Case-Buster, Spiritual Adviser, By Appointment Only." Prosecutors established a link between this self-proclaimed storefront minister and con man and Lawrence Horn. The two men had been introduced in 1992 through Thomas Turner of Detroit, Horn's first cousin and Perry's friend. Testifying under a grant of immunity, Turner said Horn had confided that he was frustrated over an ongoing custody battle with his wife, Mildred, and told Turner he needed someone to help. During the next year, Turner acted as a go-between, helping the two men communicate in a number of calls using public telephones. Turner said, however, that he began to become suspicious of their intent. After reading the news headlines about the 1993 murders of the Horn family in Maryland, Turner said he immediately disassociated himself from the two accused conspirators.

During the five-week trial, prosecutors presented details demonstrating the defendant's meticulous planning. Telephone records showed seventy calls between Horn's Los Angeles home and a pay phone near Perry's home in Detroit, as well as sixty-six calls from pay phones near Horn's home to Perry's residence. Travel records confirmed that Perry made three reconnaissance trips to Montgomery County before the killings, and he was registered at a hotel near the crime scene on the day before the murders. He also called Horn in California soon after the murders, from a public phone in Maryland.

Although there was no physical evidence connecting Perry to the crimes, prosecutors pointed out that the procedures followed at the crime scene matched twenty-two points of instruction found in a book titled *Hit Man: A Technical Manual for Independent Contractors*. Perry had ordered the assassination manual—as well as *How to Make Disposable Silencers*—from the publisher Paladin Press in Boulder, Colorado. Prosecutors said the amateur assassin had used the 138-page murder manual as a blueprint for the killings, down to the .22-caliber AR-7 murder weapon. Police later recovered pieces of the broken rifle along a roadside ditch, not far from the crime scene. Besides having filed down the serial number, Perry also had scratched the inside of the barrel to mislead authorities—both actions recommended by the author of the *Hit Man* manual. According to a *Washington Post* article, prosecutors also suggested that a cassette tape recording, found on the answering machine in Horn's Los Angeles home, was of a phone call Perry had made at 5:12 A.M. eastern time on the day of the murders. The garbled-sounding message seemed to indicate that the accused killer was offering to take a picture of Trevor in his bed and had made reference to "the noise," which apparently was the alarm connected to the disabled boy's bed that was activated when he stopped breathing.

Witnesses said that the few times Lawrence Horn returned to Maryland from California, he was not allowed in Mildred's home. During a 1992 visit, however, he videotaped the outside of his ex-wife's residence. His daughter Tiffani testified she had videotaped her brother Trevor in his room at her father's request using his camcorder. But, she added, she refused to tape the interior of the rest of the house, despite her father's request that she do so.

After five hours, the seven-woman, five-man jury found James Perry guilty of the three brutal murders, and he was later sentenced to death. This was bad news for Horn, who was still awaiting his turn to face a Maryland judge and jury.

Six months later, in April 1996, the trial of Lawrence Horn began. Much of the evidence that had condemned the hired hit man James Perry also helped convict the relative of two of the victims. Detectives also showed that Perry had received between $5,000 and $6,000 in cash, wired from an office near Horn's California home, prior to the murders. Prosecutors described Horn as a monster who hired Perry in order to inherit the $1.7 million that remained of the medical malpractice settlement. Defense attorneys argued that Horn was a loving father who was acquainted with Perry but had no part in the murders.

One of Horn's alibis was a dated and timed videotape he had made late on the night before the killings. In his apartment, located 3,000 miles from the murders that would take place only a few hours later, the down-on-his-luck record producer captured images of himself and his girlfriend watching late-night television in California. Apparently this attempt to distance himself from the heinous crimes committed by his accomplice had no effect on the jury.

In early May, Horn was found guilty of all charges. Unlike Perry, however, he was sentenced to three life sentences with no chance of parole for his role in the murders. After the sentencing was announced, Tiffani Horn, the defendant's daughter, looked at her father and said tearfully, "I hate you. I hate you so much. You killed my family." One of Mildred's siblings expressed her family's disappointment with the verdict, as they were hoping the ex-husband would receive the death penalty.

Following the hit man's appeal in 2001, Perry's death sentence was reduced to three life terms in prison with no chance of parole. The defense expressed relief that the killer had escaped the death penalty, but family members of the victims again left the courtroom disappointed.

Further developments associated with the "Hit Man" case soon made national headlines, however, when members of the Horn and Saunders families sued Paladin Press, charging that the step-by-step murder manual "aided and abetted" in the Maryland killings.

Established in 1970, Paladin Press published a number of titles that critics described as how-to instruction manuals on committing crime. Others considered the company's volumes on self-defense and survival skills both informational and practical, and supporters claimed the books were protected by the First Amendment. Still, such titles as *Contingency Cannibalism: Superhardcore Survivalism's Dirty Little Secrets* caused some to wonder about the type of clientele the publisher was seeking to attract.

Initially, as reported in the *Baltimore Sun*, a Maryland federal district judge dismissed the case on the grounds that book publishers are protected by the First Amendment and don't forfeit their rights "simply because the publication of an idea creates a potential hazard." Despite that ruling, the survivors of the victims, with the support of several victims-rights groups, appealed the decision. A three-judge panel of the Fourth Circuit Court of Appeals later ruled in the plaintiffs' favor, saying the publisher could be held liable on the grounds that "Perry had 'meticulously followed' Paladin's book in committing the three murders."

This ruling set the stage for a controversial trial. It also spawned a series of thoughtful and attention-grabbing articles and opinion columns in national publications, written by free-speech advocates and constitutional scholars, as well as representatives of the publishing industry. This last group was particularly interested in the case and, depending on the outcome, feared how far the results of the proceeding would reach. In a *New York Times* article with the attention-grabbing headline "Lawsuit Tests Lethal Power of Words," James Brooke focused on the controversy involving free speech in a piece that included excerpts from his interview with Peter C. Lund, the former Green Beret captain who owned Paladin Press.

In May 1999, within a week of the start of the trial, the publisher settled the federal lawsuit filed by the victims' families. In the out-of-court settlement, Paladin Press agreed to stop selling the book and pay millions of dollars to the plaintiffs. An attorney for the families noted that the publisher also agreed to make donations to two charities, remove *Hit Man* from its catalog, and cease publication of the book. A lawyer representing Hollywood movie studios, TV producers, and book publishers admitted to the Associated Press that the impending case "was making the entertainment industry nervous."

But Paladin's *Hit Man* headaches weren't over. In February 2002, the Boulder publisher settled another pending lawsuit, this one filed by an Oregon woman who in 1998 had fought off a hired killer. During the trial, it was learned that the woman's husband had hired the attacker, who admitted to using a Paladin Press book as his guide. The plaintiff originally sought at least $4.5 million in damages from the publisher, no doubt encouraged by the successful outcome of the lawsuit filed by the families of the "Hit Man" murder victims. Details of the Oregon settlement with the publisher were not disclosed. The woman's husband and his hired attacker were sentenced in 1999 to more than seventeen years in prison.

CHAPTER 8
Internet Death Wish

✳ ✳ ✳

The rural community of Hampstead, Maryland, is not much more than a dot on a map. Located near the Maryland-Pennsylvania border of the Mason-Dixon line, it's only about a forty-five-minute drive northwest of Baltimore. Hampstead is a place folks pass through on their way to somewhere else or, if lost, stop to ask a local for directions.

Like many other East Coast villages, it traces its roots to a tavern that served as a stagecoach stop. Some history books claim Hampstead was the site of America's first one-room schoolhouse, and reports of mysterious tunnels beneath a few older homes generated tales of Underground Railroad connections and links with the Civil War. But most agree that nothing of earthshaking historical significance ever occurred there. Hampstead was just a pleasant, off-the-beaten-track village surrounded by newer bedroom developments where commuters lived the quiet life, away from traffic, tourists, news cameras, and controversy.

But the area's quiet ambience changed suddenly in the fall of 1996, when a tale of sordid sex, trailer park torture, a grisly murder, and affairs conducted through online chat rooms earned the sleepy hideaway national headlines and hours of cable news coverage—all revolving around the secret Internet world of Sharon Lopatka.

To neighbors and professional associates, the thirty-five-year-old, five-foot ten-inch, 189-pound Carroll County woman was an average, happily married homemaker and businesswoman who worked from her home office. Born Sharon Denburg, she grew up in a strict Baltimore Jewish family that took its religious heritage and traditions seriously. As a young woman, Sharon was raised in Maryland's largest city, leading an ordinary life. She played on high school sports teams, worked in the library, and sang in the school chorus. At age twenty-nine, Sharon married Victor Lopatka, despite her family's strong protests. They disapproved of their daughter's relationship with Victor because he was a gentile and a Catholic.

For six years, the Lopatka couple lived a seemingly pleasant and uneventful life. Sharon operated several businesses over the Internet and, in cooperation with a neighbor, produced a small how-to booklet on creating country crafts and home decorating tips. The two authors sold their product at fund-raisers, ladies' group gatherings, and church events.

In newspaper stories, neighbors and friends interviewed by various reporters described Lopatka as "just like anyone else" and "about as normal as you can get." There was no indication that anyone suspected her involvement in the sordid and secretive world of cyberspace, where she spent a considerable amount of her time.

Most of Lopatka's businesses were rather conventional—offering instructions on how to make money through advertisements and selling information about income-producing offers using telephone 900 numbers. Lopatka also earned money rewriting Internet advertisements through another of her operations, called Classified Concepts

Unlimited. But the nature of some of Lopatka's other Internet enterprises apparently led her into the seedy world of mysterious chat rooms, where online conversations among unseen strangers focused on bondage, domination, and sadomasochism.

Psychics Know All and Dionne Enterprises, two of Lopatka's other websites, offered fortune-telling advice provided by Vilado, "America's Favorite Warlock." Although described as a "powerful mystic," this gifted wizard apparently was nothing more than an imaginary creation. Using the mysterious character, Lopatka sought to entice gullible customers, who were promised advice and details on securing cures or curses—all available for a fee.

But when her business responsibilities were concluded, Lopatka delved further into what the Internet had to offer, entering a world where anonymity allowed her to assume dramatically different identities—with new names, appearances, occupations, and desires.

With a tap on her keyboard, the heavyset suburban businesswoman transformed herself into Miranda, a five-foot six-inch, 121-pound, stunning beauty offering her worn undergarments for a price. Another click of her mouse and she was Nancy Carlson, an attractive pornographic video star who marketed customized sexual videos, based on each buyer's specific desires. Moments later, Lopatka would erase these roles and assume her third persona, Gina108, a 300-pound dominatrix with an aggressive personality. It was while playing this character that Lopatka wrote: "DO YOU DARE ENTER . . . THE LAND OF THE GIANTESS??? Where men are crushed like bugs . . . by this angry . . . yet gorgeous giant goddess."

For months, Lopatka trolled the amorphous realms of cyberspace, seeking to attract the attention of the right people. But it was a message she posted in August 1996 that generated the most interest and subsequent responses from online chat room readers. In fact, several of the veteran players in the Internet netherworld wondered how serious Gina108 was, and just how far she was really willing to go in pursuit of her bizarre fantasy.

"Hi my name is Gina . . . I kind of have a fascination with torturing till death . . . of course, I can't speak about it with my friends or family. Would love to have an e-mail exchange with someone."

According to the *Washington Post*, this message caught the attention of Tanith Tyrr, a "sex rights advocate" from Berkeley, California. Tyrr told that newspaper that after Lopatka accessed various chat rooms stating she was interested in being "tortured to death," several male readers corresponded with "Gina." But they all ceased contact upon discovering she was quite serious about using the Internet to effect her own demise.

Tyrr told *Post* reporters Doug Struck and Fern Shen that her attempts to counsel Lopatka over the Internet were rejected. Lopatka responded, 'I want to surrender completely. I want to die.' She was trying to get in the [bondage] community to find someone who would do it for real. I wrote her and even sent her information trying to show her there is a difference between fantasy and reality."

"I want the real thing. I didn't ask for you preaching to me," Tyrr said Lopatka had replied in response to the Californian's well-intentioned advice.

On October 13, two months after Lopatka had posted her attention-grabbing death wish on the Internet, she drove from her Carroll County home to downtown Baltimore. After parking her Honda Civic at Amtrak Penn Station on North Charles Street, she boarded the 9:15 A.M. southbound train, heading for an appointment in Charlotte, North Carolina. Her husband thought she was going away for a few days to visit with friends in Georgia.

Twelve hours later, at 9 P.M., Robert Glass, age forty-five, was waiting to meet Lopatka for the first time in person. They had communicated heavily during the previous two months through an Internet chat room. Lopatka climbed into Glass's beat-up pickup truck and rode with the stranger to Caldwell County, where he lived in a turquoise trailer in a rural area about seventy-five miles from Charlotte.

Glass was very knowledgeable about computers and the Internet, having worked for more than fifteen years as a computer analyst and programmer for the government of neighboring Catawba County. He spent his days in a basement office, tabulating statistics for the county's voter registration system and tracking the gas consumption of the jurisdiction's motor vehicle fleet. During the nights, he sat alone in front of his glowing computer screen and delved into his obsession—sending sexual messages and sordid images from his trailer to like-minded chat room visitors located around the world.

He had connected with Lopatka in August. In the two months before she headed south to meet her mystery man, the online couple had exchanged nearly nine hundred pages of email correspondence. Sharon's chat room identity was Nancy. Glass went by a more mysterious moniker, Slowhand.

While Sharon was in North Carolina, Victor Lopatka began wondering about the whereabouts of his wife. On October 20, a week after she had left home, he discovered a note from Sharon resting near her computer. In it, she stated that she was not returning home and said, "If my body is never retrieved, don't worry, know that I am at peace." She added that her husband should not to try to seek out her killer.

After Victor called the Maryland State Police, investigators arrived at the Lopatka home. Following an examination of Sharon's computer, police sifted through hundreds of messages and discovered a direct connection to Glass, including the arrangements to meet with him on the evening of October 13 in a North Carolina train station.

Six months earlier, Robert "Bobby" Glass had become separated from his wife, Sherri. The couple, who had been married fourteen years, had two girls and a boy. Sherri said she had left her husband because he ignored her and spent virtually all of his free time on the computer. One day while he was at work, she went online and discovered her husband's visits to sordid chat rooms. When she saw the content of some of his email chat sessions, she became very disturbed and realized she did not really know the man with whom she had been living.

By October 25, police in both Maryland and North Carolina had gathered considerable evidence from the lengthy email correspondence between Lopatka and Glass—in which Slowhand "described in detail how he was going to sexually torture and, ultimately, kill her." Armed with a search warrant, members of the Caldwell County Sheriff's Department entered Glass's trailer, near the town of Lenoir, North Carolina, while he was at work.

Investigators were repulsed by what they found inside the worn metal structure. Trash and debris were interspersed among materials related to sex and bondage. Police collected thousands of computer discs, some containing child pornography. There also were items identified as belonging to Lopatka.

The *Washington Post* reported that one officer searched the grounds and, about eighty feet from the trailer, stumbled on a fresh, shallow grave, which appeared to have just been dug. Lopatka's dead body was resting inside the pit. Police said that if the corpse had been deposited a few feet farther, beyond the nearby wood line in the adjacent forest, Lopatka's remains might not have been discovered during the initial search. Because the victim was significantly heavier than Glass, it was believed he was unable to drag her limp body any farther.

The dead and bruised body was deposited only two and a half feet below the surface. Lopatka's hands and feet had been tied with rope, and a nylon cord had been tightened around her neck. Scratches were found on other parts of the decomposing corpse.

Autopsy results indicated that Lopatka had died of strangulation on October 16, only three days after her arrival at Glass's residence. Apparently the victim had remained voluntarily in Glass's trailer each day while the accused was at work. The couple, who had met through the Internet, engaged in their bizarre and violent sexual fantasies each night—until things went too far.

But after reading through hundreds of pages of email correspondence detailing their sexual interests and plans, police believed Lopatka had boarded the train in Baltimore fully expecting, after she reached her preplanned destination, to be abused, painfully tortured, and finally, killed. In an Associated Press story in the *Augusta Chronicle*, Capt. Danny Barlow of the Caldwell County Sheriff's Department said: "If you put all their messages together, you'd have a very long novel. It would be very thick, and I think you could say it would have a very sad ending."

Glass admitted to tying up Lopatka, but he said it was part of their mutual interest to help her climax during intercourse. He said her death by strangulation was accidental. His lawyer, Neil Beach, argued against the state's contention that Glass was a cold-blooded, calculating, premeditated killer. But the state countered that Glass's emails, composed and transmitted using his pseudonym, Slowhand, provided substantial evidence that the killing was well planned and thought out in advance. The state charged Glass with first-degree murder.

In "All about Sharon Lopatka," posted on crimelibrary.com, Rachel Bell noted, "According to Capital News Service, the Lopatka case was the first time a police unit captured a murder suspect based primarily on evidence obtained from e-mail messages."

Since the case had generated significant national attention, experts, interested citizens, and television viewers began to present their reactions, with many condemning the easily accessible evils offered through the Internet. This brought out an equal number of avid computer users, who claimed the World Wide Web was nothing more than a marvelous tool that individuals could decide to use wisely or not.

As a result of the Lopatka–Glass case, some members of the public were introduced to a new role-playing practice, labeled the "Mardi Gras phenomenon." This term, used in American psychology, referred to a person's ability to hide, or mask, one's identity while using the Internet.

In a 2005 article in *Web Mystery Magazine*, Dr. Maurice Godwin, an assistant professor of justice studies at Methodist College in Fayetteville, North Carolina, wrote: "Outsiders may question whether individuals are able to maintain their touch with reality when they continuously pretend to be someone that they are not. This might be true for some; for others, this also means exploring their fantasies in ways never before possible." Godwin described Lopatka as "someone who trolled the Internet, little knowing someone was trolling for her, someone who had bought into the Mardi Gras effect knowingly, and with deadly intent."

On a less academic level, in 1997, a year following Lopatka's much-publicized murder, nationally known advice columnist Ann Landers made some disparaging remarks about the Internet. That column generated a significant number of angry responses from a number of her readers, who offered glowing accolades about its usefulness in sharing information, enhancing personal communication, providing medical advice, and opening up the user's eyes to travel destinations far from one's home.

Ms. Landers responded by printing a summary of an Associated Press news story spotlighting the Maryland–North Carolina "Mardi Gras" murder. In three short paragraphs, the experienced columnist described Sharon Lopatka as a married woman who was "well-liked" and "friendly," but led a secret life seeking bondage and torture through contacts on the Internet.

She mentioned Robert Glass's membership in the Rotary Club and described him as someone who was "into computers." Landers also noted the pair's nine hundred personal email messages, their secret rendezvous, and the discovery of Lopatka's corpse in a shallow grave located only seventy-five feet from Glass's front door.

Ending her column, and responding to her critics, Landers wrote, "The Rev. Clarence Widener, who officiated at Glass' wedding 15 years ago, said, 'He was a nice fellow. I don't know what could have happened to him.'"

In January 2000, Glass pleaded guilty to the voluntary manslaughter of Sharon Lopatka. Police dropped the murder charge. The killer was sentenced to three to five and a half years in prison for Lopatka's death. Glass also was sentenced to another two years in prison for possession of child pornography.

After earning credit for the three years he had spent in jail awaiting trail, Glass was scheduled to be freed from North Carolina's Avery–Mitchell Correctional Institution on March 4, 2002. Other factors, such as the state's sentencing-structure rules and Glass's good conduct—having maintained a spotless prison record, with no rule infractions during his confinement—were taken into consideration as the state prepared for the killer's early release.

But on February 19, the Watauga County medical examiner pronounced Robert Frederick Glass, fifty-one, formerly of Lenoir, North Carolina, dead of a heart attack—just two weeks short of his scheduled release from prison.

CHAPTER 9
Beltway Snipers

✳ ✳ ✳

The snipers' first bullet missed. Unfortunately, their subsequent shots hit their targets, resulting in a twenty-three-day period of terror that affected residents living in areas surrounding the District of Columbia, one of the most populated regions in the country. During more than three tense weeks in the fall of 2002, frustrated law enforcement personnel representing federal agencies, local communities, and several states devoted innumerable hours to trying to capture the elusive shooters. But the perpetrators seemed almost invisible, leaving a random trail of murdered and injured bodies in their wake. And members of a terrorized public wondered if they or someone they knew would be the next target locked in the snipers' sights.

At 5:20 P.M. on Wednesday, October 2, at the end of the workday, a bullet crashed through the glass of one of the large front windows of a Michaels arts and crafts store, located in a strip mall in Aspen Hill. The Montgomery County retail outlet in Northgate Plaza was similar to thousands of other hobby shops in shopping centers scattered across the country. Its low-priced imported items attracted a faithful clientele of homemakers, teachers, and hobbyists interested in purchasing inexpensive supplies to create decorative items and school projects. It wasn't the kind of place that typically drew the attention of robbers, gang members, delinquents, or troublemakers, as might a liquor outlet, nightclub, or twenty-four-hour convenience store.

The cashier at aisle number 5 heard a crash and felt a rush of wind, as an unseen flying object seemed to pass near her station. The projectile turned out to be a .223-caliber bullet, which lodged itself in a rear wall of the store. With no other clues or witnesses, investigating detectives considered the possibilities—an accidental discharge or a missed intentional shot. Although the bullet could have been aimed at the employee, the probability seemed slight. Since there was not enough information for the experts to make a definitive decision, the reason for the shooting, and the identity of the shooter, would remain a mystery—for the time being.

Within less than an hour, James D. Martin, an analyst for the National Oceanic and Atmospheric Association, was shot while walking through the parking lot of a Shoppers Food Warehouse store in Wheaton, about two miles from the Michaels store. The fifty-five-year-old husband, father, churchgoer, and school mentor was planning to pick up some items for a church youth group. The bullet entered his back, and the victim fell to the ground. Almost immediately, a Montgomery County police officer, who had been nearby and heard the shot, rushed to the crime scene. Paramedics and more officers arrived soon, but they could not save the man's life. The victim's body was taken away for examination.

Police tried to determine a motive. It was not a robbery. The shooting took place in a well-traveled, congested area during rush hour—and no one saw the shooter, nor was anyone able to identify a site from which the shot may have originated. For the second time that day, a bullet out of nowhere had attracted the attention of Montgomery County police. But they still weren't sure whether the two shootings were connected.

The next day, Thursday, October 3, Montgomery County police discovered that their jurisdiction probably was the center of a deadly crime spree. Therefore, the Michaels cashier at checkout aisle number 5 may indeed have been the shooter's first target— and luckily for her, this was one of the few times the killer would miss his prey.

The first shot that Thursday morning rang out in the midst of the morning rush hour. During the next two hours and seventeen minutes, four more murders were added to Montgomery County's list of unsolved crimes.

At 7:41 A.M., James L. "Sonny" Buchanan Jr., a thirty-nine-year-old landscaper, was killed while mowing a lawn near a car dealership in Rockville. The cause of death initially was believed to be an industrial accident, probably caused by a defective lawn mower. However, medical personnel at the hospital eventually discovered the deadly wound was caused by a bullet.

The next victim was Premkumar A. Walekar, age fifty-four, a taxicab driver who had come to America from India. Walekar was killed at 8:12 A.M., while pumping gas at a Mobil station in Aspen Hill. The site was less than a block from the Michaels store where the first shot in the area had been fired the night before.

Less than half an hour later, at 8:37, Sarah Ramos, thirty-four, was killed while sitting on a bench at a shopping center near Leisure World retirement community in Silver Spring. A house cleaner, the woman was waiting to be picked up by her employer. First reports erroneously suggested that she had committed suicide.

The final victim that morning was Lori Lewis-Rivera, a twenty-five-year-old nanny, who was killed at 9:58 A.M. while vacuuming her employer's minivan at a Shell gas station in Kensington.

As teams of police investigators raced to the multiple crime scenes, cordoned off areas, tried to gather witness statements, sought to confirm a link among the shootings, looked for motives, and worked on assembling a plan of operation, citizens in what is one of the most affluent counties in the entire country heard the news bulletins and began to wonder how safe they and their children were.

With nearly 900,000 residents, and adjacent to Washington, D.C., the heavily populated region had experienced more than its share of terror associated with 9/11 and in the months that followed. A hijacked airliner had crashed into the nearby Pentagon, and the chemical anthrax scare had closed one of the U.S. Senate office buildings. Both of these sites were military and governmental targets that were expected to be on a number of terrorists' hit lists.

But as *Washington Post* reporters Sari Horwitz and Michael E. Ruane stated in the book they coauthored, *SNIPER: Inside the Hunt for the Killers Who Terrorized the Nation*: "The sniper attacks were entirely different. The targets had been selected at random and slaughtered for maximum shock effect . . . The public got the message: It could be anybody. It could be me. Much more so than with 9/11 or anthrax, the terror was real, and it was spreading."

As a joint operation task force was being organized, detectives brainstormed, and forensic scientists studied bullet fragments, the public reacted to a series of worsening news reports. Schools were placed in lockdown mode. Outdoor public events were canceled. And citizens began to consider the deadly consequences that could occur as they did such simple tasks as going shopping, filling up gas tanks, or visiting an outdoor ATM. Meanwhile, whoever was responsible for the shootings seemed to be able to move about freely, taking advantage of the confusion and panic that had arisen in less than a day in the congested and usually peaceful region.

The killer wasn't done for the day, however. At 9:15 P.M. on October 3, at an intersection on the edge of Washington, a seventy-two-year-old man named Pascal Charlot became the day's fifth victim. The Haitian immigrant and carpenter was planning to cross the street when he was shot. At first police thought he might be the victim of everyday gun violence such as occurred in the nation's capital, but authorities soon realized that the sniper was not limiting his attacks to daylight hours.

Many questioned how a shooter could pull a trigger that generated a loud rifle crack and then seem to evaporate into thin air without being noticed—particularly with thousands of law enforcement personnel and concerned citizens increasingly aware of the deadly situation and on the lookout for the slightest sign of unusual behavior.

* * *

What turned out to be an erroneous report of a "white box van" racing from the scene of one of the first shootings caused frustrated investigators, the competitive and hungry members of the growing press corps, and an increasingly frightened public to focus their attention in the wrong direction. This mistake, with everyone concentrating on the wrong type of vehicle, allowed a dark blue 1990 Chevrolet Caprice with tinted windows to become almost invisible and slip through the series of ever-widening police dragnets.

Inside the large Chevy sedan, which had a spacious trunk and sported New Jersey license plates, were John Allen Muhammad (originally John Allen Williams), forty-one, a Gulf War army veteran, auto repairman, convert to Islam, and all-around con man; and Lee Boyd Malvo, a seventeen-year-old Jamaican boy who first met Muhammad in Antigua and was later reunited with the elder former soldier in Fort Myers, Florida.

Muhammad had left the U.S. Army after seventeen years and lived in Tacoma, Washington. After becoming estranged from his second wife, Mildred, with whom he had three children, he settled for a time in Antigua, where he existed by selling forged documents to foreigners who wanted to enter the United States. He met Malvo through the younger man's mother, Una James, who had become friendly with Muhammad. After Una settled in Fort Myers,

Muhammad visited her. He eventually arranged to take young Malvo off her hands and under his wing. Beginning in October 2001, the two crisscrossed the country, living in several states, including Washington, where Muhammad had resided for some time and still had acquaintances. Throughout their journey, and wherever they stopped to live for short periods of time, the duo passed themselves off as father and son.

While staying in YMCAs and homeless shelters out west, Muhammad caught up with some former military buddies. In July 2002, he stole a Bushmaster XM-15—the weapon he and Malvo eventually used in the East Coast killings—from Bull's Eye Shooter Supply, a Tacoma gun shop. The Gulf War veteran also practiced his marksmanship and the effectiveness of a homemade silencer by shooting at a tree stump behind the Washington State home of an old army friend, Robert Holmes. Later Holmes said he remembered Muhammad referring to Malvo as his "little sniper."

The two men's trip back to the East Coast may have been made partly to harass Muhammad's second ex-wife, who had moved to Clinton, Maryland, south of Washington, D.C. On September 5, a month before the snipers fired their first shot in Montgomery County, Paul LaRuffa, owner of an Italian restaurant, was shot and wounded in his parking lot in Clinton. The assailant, who used a .22-caliber pistol, got away with $3,500 in cash and a laptop computer. It wasn't until after the snipers' capture that police learned of their connection to that crime and how, along with the stolen money, the laptop had served as a high-tech tool to aid them in their three-week string of murders.

In the immediate aftermath of the first two days of East Coast killings, many regional residents had begun to develop a new habit: watching unscheduled press conferences conducted by Charles Moose, Montgomery County police chief. The county's top law enforcement officer had become a recognizable presence on televised updates, through which he informed an increasingly tense populace on the rapidly changing developments related to the shootings. After all, Montgomery County had been considered a safe community. During the first three quarters of 2002, there had been only twenty reported murders. Overnight, the law enforcement community had seen its homicide rate increase by 25 percent.

The chief appealed for calm and asked for assistance, stating he believed that someone had seen something that would help the investigation. Moose urged the public to come forward with whatever information it might have. To the press and the public, it was apparent that law enforcement was seeking any assistance it could get, and that those charged with catching the shooter were as much in the dark as the average citizen regarding the killer's identity, motives, and next moves.

Since the rapid succession of shootings had occurred north of the nation's capital, most experts assumed that any additional attack would happen in that same area. Other communities in the region did not expect their citizens to also become targets—until 2:27 P.M. on Friday, October 4, in Fredericksburg, Virginia, seventy-five miles to the south.

At the Spotsylvania Mall near I-95, Caroline Seawell was shot while loading packages into her minivan. She had been shopping at the Michaels store there. Luckily, her injury was not fatal, and the victim would survive. One witness recalled seeing a dark car with a New Jersey license plate leaving the parking lot.

Because of the similarities to the Maryland shootings, law enforcement personnel assumed the crime was the work of the same sniper, and that he had extended his stalking area far beyond his initial territory. Members of the Montgomery County task force flew by helicopter to the crime scene to obtain information from and share details with Virginia authorities.

Three days later, on Monday, October 7, the region was shocked when a thirteen-year-old eighth-grader, Iran Brown, was shot and wounded at 8:09 A.M. The incident occurred immediately after he was dropped off from his aunt's car at Benjamin Tasker Middle School in Bowie, Maryland.

In two consecutive instances, the shooter had hit his target but not delivered a fatal shot. For two families and the public, this was the first shred of anything approaching good news. Following the incident at the school, Chief Moose announced that the shooter was "stepping over the line" by targeting children. Officials raised the reward for information leading to the capture of the sniper to $200,000. Because this crime had occurred in Prince George's County, another jurisdiction was added to the growing list of agencies and personnel involved in and affected by the perplexing case.

During the search of the area surrounding Brown's school, a search dog and handler discovered a tarot card depicting the symbol of Death, a skeleton wearing a coat of armor astride a white horse and carrying a black flag. At the top edge of the card were the words "Call me God." On the back were the phrases "For you mr. Police" at the top, "Code: Call me God" in the middle, and "Do not release to the press" along the base. Authorities decided it was a sign the sniper was attempting to make contact and open a channel of communication, which they hoped would lead to the end of the crisis. But that was only wishful thinking.

Two days later, on Wednesday, October 9, in Prince William County, Virginia, not far from the Civil War battlefield known as both Bull Run and Manassas, a driver pulled into a gas station. The sound of a shot broke through the air at 8:10 P.M. at Battlefield Sunoco, not far from I-66. Dean Harold Meyers, fifty-three, a Vietnam veteran and civil engineer, was killed by a bullet wound to the head while pumping gas. This type of crime was unusual in that county. Officials knew it was the work of the killer they now referred to as the Beltway Sniper.

At 9:28 A.M. on Friday, October 11, at the Four Mile Fork Exxon station in Massaponax, Virginia, Kenneth H. Bridges, fifty-three, a businessman from Philadelphia, was heading home and stopped to fill up his tank. He had called his wife to tell her he was on his way. Shortly afterward, he was shot in the back. A state trooper who was working nearby heard the shot and rushed to Bridges' side, but the wound was fatal. Local police, the FBI, and members of the original task force flooded the scene. But once again, the shooter had disappeared.

Police hoped that a long-overdue call to the tip line would yield breakthrough results. But the equipment and personnel handling the growing number of incoming calls—ranging from false confessions to suggestions from crackpots to tips from well-intentioned citizens—were overloaded. At times, more than 25,000 calls a day were coming into the center. Overwhelmed staff did their best to prioritize leads and direct them to the appropriate sections, to be followed up as soon as possible by field investigators. Police also tracked down area rifle owners whose registered weapons shot the caliber of bullets used in the killings. Owners of gun shops were interviewed and asked to share the identities of anyone who had purchased weapons or ammunition and may have stood out by appearing unusually odd or nervous.

Meanwhile, Muhammad and Malvo traveled the region in their blue former police cruiser. With the aid of their stolen laptop, and by watching continuous television reports, the duo observed frustrated police trying to respond to every move the killers had decided to make. What would amaze authorities after the pair's capture is the number of times their suspicious car with New Jersey plates and tinted windows had been stopped and the occupants queried by police. On several other occasions, passing patrol officers had taken notice of the killers' vehicle, checked it through their computer system, and found no reason to pull the car over and question its occupants—who were planning their next killing behind the cover of their dark glass barrier.

When three days had passed without a shooting, authorities began to wonder if the sniper had moved on and left the area permanently. If so, police realized, the shooter would probably escape and never be caught. The sad reality was that the region would have to suffer through additional shootings in order for police to get enough information and evidence to make a capture.

The next murder occurred at 9:15 P.M. on Monday, October 14, in the parking lot of a Home Depot in Fairfax County, Virginia. The victim, Linda Franklin, forty-seven, an analyst for the FBI, was killed while she and her husband were loading a shelf into their car. This time someone immediately came forward and claimed to have witnessed the shooter, describing him as a man with a mustache carrying an AK-47 type weapon. He also said the shooter was driving a light-colored Chevy van with a ladder rack on the roof.

* * *

At last, police thought, they had gotten their first break in the case. Based on the timely eyewitness account, authorities issued the critical information to officers and the public. Police threw out a wide dragnet and set up search checkpoints throughout the surrounding area. News helicopters showed late-night TV viewers long lines of stopped traffic and flashing police cars along major highways.

But two days later, after continued questioning of the purported witness, a detective reviewing surveillance tapes of the store identified the man as having been inside the building—nowhere near the crime scene—at the time of the shooting. He had never been in the parking lot and therefore would not have been able to see or hear the shooting. When confronted with the information, the supposed witness admitted he had been lying. The disappointed public and always skeptical news media began to openly question the competence of those in charge of the deadlocked investigation.

Police again requested the public's help, suggesting drivers keep writing implements at hand in their vehicles to note unusual activity or record the license number of a suspicious car or van. People started walking in staggered spurts, avoiding straight-line routes. Gas stations erected large, plastic, tentlike barriers around their pump areas. Schools canceled outdoor recreation periods, and some parents kept their children home from classes. Others dropped youngsters off at school to avoid having them wait in the open at bus stops. Police recommended that people carry supplies and blankets in their automobiles, in the event they were stopped in a hastily erected roadblock. And members of groups such as the Black Panthers and Guardian Angels volunteered to pump gas for nervous patrons. After two weeks of unpredictable terror, the snipers had disrupted the routines of individuals and business operations throughout the Beltway region.

While police were hoping desperately for a break, leads continued to arrive at the call center hot line and on phone lines at various police departments in Maryland and Virginia. According to Horwitz and Ruane's book *SNIPER*, more than 80,000 tips were received by authorities. The telephone lines and workers taking calls were swamped. That's why two very important calls were lost or delayed.

In Tacoma, Washington, Robert Holmes, like most people in the country, was aware of the continuing series of random killings occurring on the East Coast. Holmes had not seen his old army friend Muhammad and his young partner, Malvo, for several months. He heard a news reporter mention that the killing might be the work of a team, involving a spotter and a shooter. And when a picture of a Bushmaster rifle, the weapon authorities said might be the model being used by the killers, was shown on TV, Holmes recalled that Muhammad owned a similar rifle. He also remembered that Muhammad had tried to adapt his rifle with a silencer and had practice fired the Bushmaster into a tree stump in Holmes's backyard.

Holmes picked up his phone and called the FBI hot line on Thursday, October 17. The report was taken and passed on for review. But it was nearly a week before investigators processed the information and conducted an interview with the caller from Washington.

Meanwhile, a day later, on Friday, October 18, Lee Malvo called the Rockville (Maryland) City Police Department from a pay phone at a gas station off I-95 in Virginia. He was attempting to establish communication and begin a dialogue that would announce the pair's ransom demand. Unaware that she was speaking to the most sought-after criminal in the country, the local police force dispatcher tried to direct the caller to the proper authorities who were operating the case. As she tried to give Malvo the number for the hot line, the frustrated shooter hung up.

Not giving up, the snipers made a second call late that afternoon. This time, when Montgomery County police officer Derek Baliles answered his phone, the caller referred to the sniper killings. In an attempt to establish his bona fides, the caller told the officer to call Sergeant Marina at the Montgomery (Alabama) Police Department and inquire about the shooting and robbery at a liquor store that had

EXECUTIONS IN MARYLAND

As one of the nation's earliest settlements, it is not surprising that Maryland has a long history of capital punishment, extending back nearly 350 years. Initially, the most common form of capital punishment was hanging. As technologies advanced, public awareness increased, and sensibilities changed, methods employed to rid society of its most dangerous convicted criminals were modified. In later years, the gas chamber was employed, and finally, the method of choice in most states became lethal injection—believed to be less painful, more reliable, and therefore more humane.

In nearly every society and time period, murder has been considered the most repulsive crime and the one most deserving of the death penalty. "Under the provisions of an early Maryland statute any one convicted of murder could be put to death and all his property confiscated," Raphael Semmes reported in *Crime and Punishment in Early Maryland*, although there were "comparatively few indictments for murder in proprietary Maryland and even fewer executions for this crime."

One of the earliest applications of the death sentence occurred in the seventeenth century in St. Mary's City after the murder of Mary Utie. The family's slave, Jacob, was drawn and hanged, meaning he was dragged on the ground behind the rear of a cart from the prison to the gallows. In 1664, Joseph Fincher was convicted by a jury and court of whipping to occurred in September, a month earlier. The caller told Baliles he would call back after giving the officer time to verify the information. After Baliles relayed the details to the command center, Maryland authorities contacted their Alabama counterparts and confirmed that the caller's information was accurate. Baliles waited for the return call, which came about an hour later. But in the midst of the conversation, the call was disconnected. This conversation was the first indication of a connection between the Beltway snipers and

death his servant, Jeffery Haggman, and the landowner was hanged in Anne Arundel County. John Dandy, a blacksmith, was hanged on an island in the Patuxent River for the beating death of his young servant boy, Henry Gouge. And Elizabeth Green was found guilty of throwing her illegitimate child into a fire. A witness admitted he did not actually see the crime take place, but claimed he had heard a cry "like a pig or a child" come from the flames. That testimony was good enough for the court, and Green was convicted and hanged by the sheriff in St. Mary's County.

In Baltimore in 1818, John M. Duncan, a Scottish visitor to America, witnessed the hanging of two mail robbers. From his vantage point in the prison courtyard, surrounded by a crowd of eager spectators, Duncan recalled: "I had in my pocket a small perspective glass, which I offered to two young ladies who happened to stand near me. They seemed quite pleased with the accommodation and continue to use it alternately till the whole melancholy scene was over. The bodies on being cut down were immediately buried in the corner of the prison yard."

As time passed, other forms of entertainment became available, and the public's interest in witnessing executions waned. According to the Maryland Department of Public Safety website, the first indoor hanging occurred in January 1913, in the Baltimore City Jail, with only invited witnesses present. With a change in the state law in 1923, all Maryland executions were carried out within the walls of the prison. George Chelton, a

(continued on page 110)

twenty-one-year-old Somerset County convicted rapist, was the first person hanged in this nonpublic setting in June of that year. Over the next twenty-three years, state records report, "75 men stepped onto the gallows, with 12 double and two triple hangings taking place."

Well-known Baltimore newspaperman H. L. Mencken witnessed and reported on nine hangings. In an August 16, 1926, *Baltimore Sun* column, he shared his observations on crime, punishment, and the benefits of execution by hanging: "It is my firm impression that this operation, if competently carried out, is a humane method of putting criminals to death, though perhaps it is not quite as quick as electrocution." Mencken believed the overwhelming percentage of the public supported the death penalty for anyone who selected "murder as his trade."

Not every hanging was reported in detail, but the unusual gallows experience of Jack Johnson, convicted of a double murder, warranted headline-grabbing newspaper ink. Soon after midnight on June 30, 1930, the convicted murdered heard the switch being thrown, fell through the trapdoor—but, to his and everyone's surprise, landed on the ground below. The cause of the botched execution was a broken rope. According to the Maryland state website on capital punishment history: "His limp form was quickly placed on a stretcher and carried up on the scaffold where his neck was put into a fresh noose. With Johnson still supported by the stretcher, the trap was sprung again, and he was pronounced dead shortly after."

a crime that had taken place in Alabama. Although the details seemed perplexing at the time, this information later proved to be a major break in the up-to-now frustrating, dead-end case.

At 7:59 P.M. on Saturday, October 19, Jeffrey and Stephanie Hopper walked across the parking lot of a Ponderosa Steakhouse in Ashland, Virginia. A shot, which witnesses said seemed to come from a wooded area, was fired as the Florida couple headed toward their car, ready to resume their trip home after having visited relatives outside Philadelphia. Fortunately, although Jeffrey was wounded, he survived.

On June 10, 1955, William C. Thomas, who had been convicted of rape and murder, became the last man to be executed by hanging in Maryland. Between that time and June 9, 1961, four criminals were asphyxiated in the state's gas chamber. Nathaniel Lipscomb, who had been convicted of rape and murder, was the last convict put to death by this method. "For 33 years after Lipscomb's execution, there were no others in Maryland," Jennifer McMenamin wrote in the *Baltimore Sun*. "The U.S. Supreme Court invalidated 40 death penalty laws across the nation in 1972, including Maryland's. The high court reinstated capital punishment in 1976. Maryland enacted new death penalty laws two years later." But Maryland courts were reluctant to seek the death penalty and nearly twenty more years would pass before another convict would enter the death chamber.

After John Thanos was convicted of murder, he became the first killer in Maryland executed by lethal injection, on May 17, 1994. Four additional men have been legally executed in Maryland since the resumption of capital punishment in 1994: Flint Gregory Hunt on July 2, 1997, for killing a Baltimore police officer; Tyrone X. Gilliam on November 16, 1998, for killing a Baltimore accountant during a robbery; Steven Howard Oken, on June 17, 2004, for the rape and murder of a White Marsh newlywed (he later also killed his sister-in-law and a motel clerk); and Wesley Eugene Baker, on December 5, 2005, for shooting a teacher's aide in front of her two grandchildren. It's estimated that Maryland legally executed more than 310 men, but no women, from its settlement in 1634 to 2005.

Police descended upon the scene, bringing along human trackers and gunpowder-sniffing dogs. An Alcohol, Tobacco and Firearms (ATF) special agent's Labrador, named Garrett, signaled to a site where searchers discovered a .223-caliber cartridge casing. Searchers also found a plastic bag attached to a tree. It was apparently from the killers, and it contained a message addressed to the police.

Several pieces of lined paper included a repetition of the original instructions that had been printed on the earlier tarot card clue—about not releasing information to the press and restating the code phrase "Call me God." The new correspondence, filled with awkward phrases and misspellings, also indicated the killers' previous attempts to make contact by phone, and the writer complained about the "incompetence" of the authorities. The writer provided a phone number and directed police to use it during future contacts. The shooters demanded $10 million, to be deposited—within two days—into the Visa account of a credit card they apparently had stolen months earlier from a Greyhound bus driver when Malvo and Muhammad had been traveling in Arizona. The killers ended the long message with two warnings: "If trying to catch us now more important then prepare you [*sic*] body bags" and "P.S. your children are not safe anywhere at any time."

Immediately, personnel from the FBI, Secret Service, the ATF, and state and local police departments rushed to analyze the wealth of information contained in the message discovered near the latest crime scene. They also made plans to catch the killers by being prepared to pinpoint the location of the expected follow-up telephone contact and set up surveillance.

But the task force decided not to share the contents of the message with the public or press. Nevertheless, some of the information contained in the note found in the Virginia woods was leaked. Two days later, on Monday morning, October 21, more than 100,000 students in five Richmond-area counties stayed home because their schools had been ordered closed. Reporters immediately wondered what Virginia school officials knew that would have caused such an unusual and unscheduled school lockout. At the same time, Maryland citizens, who were obviously in the dark about the snipers' new stated threat to children, asked if their youngsters were safe or whether their schools also had been targeted by the shooter.

Early that same morning, Malvo made a brief, thirty-eight-second call—from an Exxon station pay phone outside Richmond—to a number the police had provided previously. He instructed police to hold a press conference to give a signal that the authorities were accepting the snipers' demands. They were told to say they had "caught the sniper like a duck in a noose." And the caller added: "Your children are not safe."

Within minutes, police had tracked the incoming call and surrounded the originating area. At that moment, Jose Morales was walking across the parking lot; Edgar Rivera Garcia was talking on a pay phone while sitting in his white van. Both confused and startled men were scooped up in the preplanned, fast-moving police dragnet. But Malvo had left the scene moments earlier, and the police nabbed the wrong guys.

At 5:56 the next morning, before the start of rush hour, bus driver Conrad Johnson, thirty-five, a husband and father of two children, was standing on the steps at the doorway of his blue-and-white Montgomery County public bus. The large vehicle was stationary, ready to begin its morning route from Aspen Hill toward Bethesda.

When the bullet hit its target, the stunned victim fell onto the bus floor. A trainee who had been with the driver that morning immediately called 911. Johnson was taken to a hospital in Bethesda, where he died about three and a half hours later. The shooting location was not far from the Michaels store where the first sniper attack had taken place on October 2, nearly three weeks earlier. The executioners had returned to the site of their initial shooting.

Police searching the woods near the bus parking area discovered a plastic bag containing a note that began with the familiar salutations: "For you, Mr. Police," "Call me God," and "Do not release to the press." The shooters also repeated their previous warning: "Your children are not safe." The message stated that the lack of response to earlier demands had cost another life, and that the police should make the announcement "We have caught the sniper like a duck in a noose" to signal that authorities would meet the $10 million demand and deposit the money as instructed.

After three weeks of killings and no apparent progress, pressure on the police was mounting from several sources. Authorities were upset they had missed their chance to grab the sniper at the Richmond gas station. Chief Moose was trying to continue a veiled dialogue with the killers through public press conferences. Reporters were becoming more aggressive with their questions and increasingly frustrated at being stonewalled. And a growing number of citizens were impatient and worried that the killings would extend into the upcoming Halloween season. No one wanted parents to have to worry that their costumed children were slow-moving targets as they solicited treats while traveling from house to house. There was talk that the annual trick-or-treat custom might have to be canceled altogether or limited to indoor private parties.

* * *

Three thousand miles away, in Tacoma, Washington, on Tuesday, October 22, investigators finally visited Robert Holmes, who explained the reasons for his suspicions about Muhammad's involvement in the D.C.-area killings. Holmes also provided information about Lee Boyd Malvo, including a description of the boy, and told authorities that Muhammad's ex-wife, Mildred, lived in Maryland. Investigators also found remnants of the silencer Muhammad had attempted to build at Holmes's home.

Another development took place across the country that confirmed Holmes's suspicions. When the task force had followed up on the Alabama shooting at the urging of the sniper, Montgomery police had sent up a gun catalog they had found at the scene of the September crime. FBI experts ran fingerprints found on the publication through its database and got a match. The computer identified the prints as those of an illegal immigrant from Jamaica who had been arrested in Washington State the previous December. His name was Lee Boyd Malvo. An examination of the documents filed at the time of the boy's arrest mentioned the presence of another man—John Muhammad.

Finally the East Coast task force had received a fairly good lead, with names and faces to go along with the crimes. Events now began to move at a rapid pace. The next day, a team was sent to Washington to dig up the tree stump in Holmes's yard so FBI analysts could compare any bullets found with fragments that had been taken from the Maryland and Virginia crime scenes. Other agents tracked down both Malvo's mother and Muhammad's former wife. More investigators worked to secure photographs of the suspected killers and quickly get them into the hands of law enforcement personnel nationwide.

A search of regional police files verified several encounters with the 1990 Chevrolet Caprice with New Jersey plates that was registered to Muhammad, in which the killers had been living for several weeks.

One priority, task force personnel agreed, was to keep quiet the excavation efforts at Holmes's Tacoma backyard and try to shield the activities from the press. Police feared that any publicity of this development would alert the snipers that the law was closing in. But television networks broke into their regularly scheduled programming to show videos taken from news helicopters of firemen working to remove a tree stump from the Holmes property.

Not absolutely positive the two men were the snipers, Chief Moose continued to communicate with the killers at his press briefings. The same day the excavation was taking place in Tacoma, Moose announced that an arrest warrant was issued for John Muhammad (previously Williams) on a federal firearms charge and as a possible witness with information that might be helpful to the investigation.

Late that night, on I-70, north of Frederick, Maryland, Whitney Donahue was heading home and planned to take a break at a familiar rest stop, on the slope of South Mountain just off the major four-lane highway. He had heard broadcasts that police were advising citizens to be on the lookout for a blue Caprice with the New Jersey license plate NDA-21Z. With more than an hour to go before he reached home, he took time to write the number down, figuring it would help him stay awake on the night drive home.

It was half an hour past midnight on Thursday morning, October 24, when Donahue pulled into the rest area and noticed two cars parked in the lot. One was a dark Chevrolet Caprice with the sought-after New Jersey plate: NDA-21Z.

Nervously, Donahue dialed 911 on his cell phone. He reported the car and its license number, adding that he thought there were two individuals inside the vehicle. Some police initially didn't believe the report, since the bulletin searching for the car was only a few hours old. State troopers, SWAT teams, and authorities involved in the three-week-long investigation converged on the area by car and helicopter. Air space was restricted, prohibiting news helicopters from the area, and I-70 was closed to traffic. All the while, police officers continued telephone conversations with Donahue, checking on the status of the suspects' car and advising him to stay clear of the immediate area.

Police snipers were placed in the hills surrounding the rest stop, in case the killers tried to escape or had linked up with unknown associates. Dog teams were ready to track anyone who might try to run from the rest stop and head into the forested mountain.

Just before 3:30 A.M., a force made up of Maryland State Police, Montgomery County SWAT officers, and agents from the FBI Hostage Rescue Team surrounded and rushed the car. In less than a minute, the assault team pulled the two suspects out of the vehicle and arrested Malvo and Muhammad. The older man had been asleep in the backseat. Malvo was in the front of the car, where he was supposed to be on lookout.

✳ ✳ ✳

The killings were over, but the in-depth investigation was still in progress. Certainly, the biggest discovery inside the car was the .223-caliber Bushmaster XM15-E2S murder weapon. But other items confiscated in and near the Caprice yielded additional damning evidence. They included a Sony laptop, AT&T calling card, extra clothing, road atlas, set of walkie-talkies, shooting mittens, GPS, tools, bolt cutters, boxes of ammunition, and papers with notes, all providing critical details about the pair's activities, plans, and routes.

According to Angie Cannon in *23 Days of Terror*, the most chilling find was how the trunk of the Caprice had been transformed into a "sniper's nest." The rear seat had been modified to allow easy access so that the shooter could lie in the large trunk. Using a hole cut into the trunk lid above the keyhole, the sniper was able to extend the rifle barrel and sight on his selected target. When the killers were mobile and not moving their car into position for a shot, they stuffed a blue sock into the round opening to conceal the hole.

The vehicle, Cannon wrote, was "a shooting gallery on wheels."

In subsequent days, as investigators tagged and matched the evidence to the long series of shootings, several legal challenges and jurisdictional arguments took place to determine who would have custody of the prisoners and where they would be tried for their crimes. Considering that the killings and attacks had taken place in several locations, the killers had crossed state lines several times, and law enforcement personnel at every level were involved in the hunt, sorting out who got how much of the prisoners' hides was going to take some hard negotiations.

At a press conference held many hours later on the evening of the capture, Chief Moose, by now a familiar, nationally known figure, assured the press and citizens that the task force would continue to function, sorting evidence and information. He added, however, "We're going to let a lot of the members of the task force, the people you see here, we're going to let them go home, hug their children, hug their spouses, and just think about the fact that we continue to live in the greatest nation. So thank you all."

The $500,000 reward was divided between the two citizens who had provided critical information regarding the identity and capture of the killers. Authorities decided Robert Holmes would receive $350,000 and Whitney Donahue would get $150,000.

Ballistics tests connected the rifle found in the Caprice to eleven of the thirteen shootings. In addition, extensive examination of the weapon, computer, vehicle, and documents discovered at the arrest eventually revealed that Muhammad and Malvo had been involved in many more killings than those that were part of the highly publicized East Coast murder rampage.

Authorities believed the pair was responsible for, or possibly associated with, nine other shootings:

- The February 16 killing of Keenya Cook, in Tacoma, Washington.
- The March 19 killing of Jerry Ray Taylor on a golf course in Tucson, Arizona.
- The September 5 wounding of Paul J. LaRuffa, shot in the parking lot of his restaurant in Clinton, Maryland.
- The September 14 wounding of Rupinder Oberoi, shot near a liquor store in Silver Spring, Maryland.
- The September 15 wounding of Muhammad Rashid, shot near a liquor store in Brandywine, Maryland.
- The September 21 killing of Million A. Woldemariam, at a liquor store in Atlanta; and the killing of Claudine Lee Parker and wounding of Kellie Adams, both shot at a liquor store in Montgomery, Alabama.
- The September 23 killing of Hong Im Ballenger, at a parking lot of Beauty Depot in Baton Rouge, Louisiana.

After, in some cases, heated arguments among prosecutors representing the jurisdictions where the crimes had occurred, authorities agreed upon Virginia as the best place to try the accused. A major factor in this decision was the fact that the southern commonwealth was second only to Texas in its application of the death penalty. Maryland, where the snipers' first shots were fired and most of the series of killings had occurred, was dismissed as an initial trial venue because of the state's well-known reputation as being soft on crime and reluctant to administer the death sentence.

Both trials were held in 2003 at the eastern edge of the state—Malvo's in Chesapeake and Muhammad's in Virginia Beach—far from where the Virginia killings had occurred, in an effort to find an unbiased jury.

In March 2004, Lee Boyd Malvo was convicted and sentenced to life without parole. In May, John Muhammad was sentenced to death. The death sentence was subject to appeal. The two were also tried in Maryland, with state prosecutors explaining that their case was pursued as insurance, in the event the Virginia convictions were ever overturned. Here Malvo pleaded guilty to six murders and confessed to further killings in other states. He also testified against Muhammad. In May 2006, Muhammad was convicted of six murder counts. In the Maryland trials, both men were sentenced to six consecutive life terms without parole. Because killings possibly connected to the convicted murderers also took place in Alabama, Arizona, Georgia, Louisiana, and Washington, the killers are subject to additional trials in those states as well.

During Malvo's testimony at Muhammad's Maryland trial, the younger man said his partner's goal was to kill six people a day for thirty days in the D.C. area to terrorize the public. He also said Muhammad wanted to murder a Baltimore police officer and detonate explosive devices at the funeral, extort several million dollars from the U.S. government, and travel into Canada and recruit young homeless people, who would cross the border and "shut things down" in cities across the United States.

Islamic-oriented documents and drawings discovered in the possession of the killers, and comments made by Malvo and Muhammad to prosecutors, indicate that the killers may have been motivated by a desire to be involved with the Islamic jihad. Malvo told a Maryland state police officer "one reason for the shootings was that white people had tried to harm Louis Farrakhan, leader of the Nation of Islam," and Muhammad reportedly told Prince William County prosecutors that "America got what it deserved" on 9/11.

Bibliography

A Brief History of Crime in Maryland

Books

Brugger, Robert J. *Maryland: A Middle Temperament, 1634–1980*. Baltimore, MD: Johns Hopkins University Press, 1988.

Mills, Eric. *Chesapeake Rumrunners of the Roaring Twenties*. Centreville, MD: Tidewater Publishers, 2000.

Online Sources

"Baltimore Riot," retrieved March 24, 2008. www.civilwarhome.com/baltimoreriot.htm.

"Convicts on the Ship *York* 1739/1740," retrieved January 11, 2008. www.olivetreegenealogy.com/ships/md_york.shtml.

"Maryland Political Scandals," retrieved July 8, 2008. www.examiner.com/x-234-Baltimore-History-Examiner~y2008m6d26-Maryland-Political-Scandals?cid=exrss-Baltimore-History-Examiner.

World Wide Words. "Lynch," retrieved January 6, 2008. www.worldwidewords.org/qa/qa-lyn1.htm.

Lovers' Lane Murders

Articles

"Blood in Auto Spurs Hunt for Young Couple." *Washington Post* (September 19, 1948).

"Edwards Says Not Guilty in Double Killing." *Washington Post* (December 14, 1948).

"Girl Believed Terrorized for 6 Hrs. after Escort Died." *Washington Post* (September 24, 1948).

"Glen Burnie Killer Sentenced to Hang." *Washington Post* (June 28, 1949).

"Glen Burnie Slayer of 2 Caught, Say Md. Police." *Washington Post* (November 11, 1948).

"Man Doomed in Md. Killings Wins New Trial." *Washington Post* (February 9, 1950).

"Maryland Couple Found Slain after 3-Day Search." *Washington Post* (September 21, 1948).

"McKeldin Spares Life of Edwards, Death Sentence Is Commuted to Life Imprisonment." *Baltimore Sun* (March 27, 1952).

Morris, Richard. "Suspect Admits Glen Burnie Murders, Lane Announces." *Washington Post* (November 12, 1948).

"New Evidence in Glen Burnie Case Reported." *Washington Post* (June 1, 1949).

"New Trial Denied Edwards in Maryland Slaying Case." *Washington Post* (June 10, 1949).

"New Trial Sought." *Washington Post* (June 2, 1949).

"1000 Hunt Pair Vainly in Maryland Car Mystery." *Washington Post* (September 20, 1948).

"Police Admit Hitting Stone Wall in Auto Slaying of 2." *Washington Post* (October 3, 1948).

"Special Squad to Work on Md. Slayings." *Washington Post* (October 6, 1948).

"Twin-Slaying Suspect Denied a Third Trial." *Washington Post* (December 8, 1950).

"Verdict Lays Two Murders to Edwards." *Washington Post* (February 10, 1949).

The Smiling "Assassinator"

Articles

Chapman, William. "Wallace: I Just Can't Worry about Some Nut . . ." *Washington Post* (May 16, 1972).

Evans, Ben. "Memory of Gov. Wallace Shooting Fades." Associated Press (May 15, 2007).

Garland, Greg. "Quietly Exiting Prison, History." *Baltimore Sun* (November 10, 2007).

"George Wallace's Appointment in Laurel." *Time* (May 29, 1972).

Greider, William. "Wallace Is Shot, Legs Paralyzed; Suspect Seized at Laurel Rally." *Washington Post* (May 16, 1976).

Lamothe, Dan. "Bremer's Release Prompts Memories of Laurel's Worst Day." *Capital News Service* (November 9, 2007).

Lucier, James P., and Timothy W. Maier. "Possible Conspiracy in Wallace Attempt?" *New World Communications, Insight on the News* (November 29, 1999).

Noe, Denise. "The Attempted Assassination of George Wallace." *Crime Magazine; An Encyclopedia of Crime* (September 19, 2007).

"Wallace's Son Wants New Inquiry into 1972 Assassination Attempt." *New York Times* (December 14, 1992).

Wolf, Jim. "Nixon Sought to Tie Wallace Shooting to Democrats." Reuters (February 28, 2002).

Online Sources

"Caught on Tape: The White House Reaction to the Shooting of Alabama Governor and Democratic Presidential Candidate George Wallace," retrieved January 19, 2008. http://hnn.us/articles/45104.html.

"George Wallace Dies: Former Alabama Governor Made 2 Strong Bids for President," retrieved January 19, 2008. www.cnn.com/US/9809/14/wallace.obit/.

Pease, Lisa. "Bremer & Wallace: It's Déjà Vu All Over Again," retrieved January 19, 2008. www.ctka.net/pr599-bremer.html.

"Portrait of an Assassin: Arthur Bremer," retrieved January 19, 2008. www.pbs.org/wgbh/amex/wallace/sfeature/assasin.html.

"Wallace in the Schoolhouse Door," retrieved January 19, 2008. www.npr.org/templates/story/story.php?storyId=1294680.

Searching for a Bishop and a Sign from "The Lord"

Interview

Popkin, Darren, Chief Deputy, Sheriff's Office, Montgomery County, Maryland. July 31, 2008.

Articles

Allegood, Jerry. "Bishop Still Wanted in Family's Death: Bodies Were Found in Tyrrell County." Raleigh, NC, *News & Observer* (February 26, 2006).

Baker, Donald. "Bishop Absence Went Uninvestigated a Week." *Washington Post* (March 12, 1976).

———. "Bradford Bishop Search Leads to Southern Italy." *Washington Post* (April 19, 1979).

———. "Brutality Unsolved: The Bishop Mystery." *Washington Post* (March 1, 1986).

———. "FBI Checking Brad Bishop Search Lead in Sweden." *Washington Post* (January 4, 1979).

Baker, Donald, and Felicity Barringer. "Search for Man Central to Slayings Probe." *Washington Post* (March 10, 1976).

Baker, Donald, and Cynthia Gorney. "5 in Md. Family Found Slain: Killed in Home, Dumped in N.C.; Father Missing." *Washington Post* (March 9, 1976).

"The Bishop Murders." *Time* (March 22, 1976).

Duggan, Paul. "Where Is Brad Bishop? 30 Years Later, Md. Murder Suspect's Flight Still a Puzzle." *Washington Post* (March 2, 2006).

Duggan, Paul, and Michael E. Ruane. "Murder Scene, Good Location." *Washington Post* (February 12, 2006).

Frazier, Joseph B. "In Tiny Wash. Town, Discovery of Parachute Stirs New Buzz over Legend of D. B. Cooper." Associated Press (March 27, 2008).

Moore, Jonathan. "Old Letter Yields Clues in '76 Killings of Diplomat's Family." Associated Press (April 1, 1993).

Rasmussen, Frederick N. "After 30 Years, Bishop Killings Still a Mystery." *Baltimore Sun* (October 14, 2006).

Online Source

Eads, Brian, and Michael Welzenbach. "World's Most Wanted." *Reader's Digest, Canada*, retrieved January 5, 2008. www.readersdigest.ca/mag/1999/10/specfeat_01.html.

Julius Salsbury

Articles

Gildea, William. "Baltimore Gamblers: Betting by the Book." *Washington Post* (May 14, 2003).

Olesker, Michael. "Gambling, Guns and These Changing Crimes." *Baltimore Sun* (April 10, 1994).

Rasmussen, Frederick N. "A Life on the Fringes Vanishes into Shadows." *Baltimore Sun* (October 21, 2006).

Cop Killer

Articles

Diehl, Jackson. "Rally Backs Johnson, Raps Police." *Washington Post* (December 3, 1978).

Feinstein, John. "Adult Trial Is Set for P.G. Youth in 2 Police Slayings." *Washington Post* (October 20, 1978).

———. "A Frightened Young Suspect or Willful Killer of Officers?" *Washington Post* (November 27, 1978).

———. "Influence Letters Rile Judge." *Washington Post* (October 19, 1978).

———. "Johnson Is Given Maximum 25 Years." *Washington Post* (May 4, 1979).

———. "Jury Hears 2 Versions of Police Deaths." *Washington Post* (March 22, 1979).

———. "$1 Million Bond Set in Slayings of 2 Police Officers." *Washington Post* (June 28, 1978).

———. "Police Threaten Walkout after Johnson Verdict." *Washington Post* (April 1, 1979).

———. "Terrence Johnson Defense Fund Gets Underway." *Washington Post* (September 7, 1978).

Feinstein, John, Jonathan Mandell, and Saundra Saperstein. "Johnson Is Acquitted of Murder, Convicted of Manslaughter." *Washington Post* (April 1, 1979).

Feinstein, John, and Robert Meyers. "9-Mile Cortege Honors Fallen 'Brothers.'" *Washington Post* (June 30, 1978).

Gambrell, Kathy. "Some of Maryland's Most Notorious Crimes." Associated Press (December 31, 1999).

Jeter, Jon. "Death Sparks Mixed Reaction among Those Who Knew Convicted Killer." *Washington Post* (February 28, 1997).

———. "Johnson's Funeral Draws Hundreds." *Washington Post* (March 5, 1997).

Jeter, Jon, and Hamil Harris. "A Tale of Life on the Outside." *Washington Post* (March 2, 1997).

Meyer, Eugene. "Saga of Terrence Johnson Ends Violently." *Washington Post* (February 28, 1997).

Scheets, Gary. "Johnson's End Elicits Array of Reactions." *Washington Times* (February 28, 1997).

Scully, Sean, and Gary Scheets. "Cop-Killer Johnson Shoots Self after Heist; He Dies 19 Years after PG Slayings." *Washington Times* (February 28, 1997).

Shaver, Katherine, and Jon Jeter. "Johnson's Death a Suicide, Autopsy Shows." *Washington Post* (March 1, 1997).

"Adios" and No Regrets

Articles

Banisky, Sandy, and Michael Ollove. "Thanos Died Quietly after a Life of Fury." *Baltimore Sun* (May 18, 1994).

Cauchon, Dennis. "Killer of Three Teens Executed in Maryland; 1st Time Since '61." *USA Today* (May 17, 1994).

"Death Sentence Is Upheld for Md. Teenager's Killer." *Washington Post* (April 6, 1993).

Keary, John. "He Told Them 'Adios,' Then Fell Unconscious." *Washington Times* (May 18, 1994).

"Killer of Md. Teens Says He Wants to Defile Corpses." *Washington Post* (June 3, 1992).

"Man Guilty of 2 Md. Murders Is Convicted in Third Killing." *Washington Post* (March 17, 1992).

"Md. Fires Official for Mistakenly Releasing Prisoner." *Washington Post* (April 13, 1992).

Metzler, Kristan. "Killer's Death Too Easy, Family Complains." *Washington Times* (May 18, 1994).

Sarris, Marina. "A Life of Crime: From Reform School to Prison, Thanos' Past Full of Violence." *Baltimore Evening Sun* (September 28, 1990).

Small, Glenn. "Murderer's Life as Abused Child Recalled at Hearing: Thanos' 'Sadistic' Father Beat Him, Social Worker Says." *Baltimore Sun* (January 29, 1992).

———. "Thanos Called a 'Menace to Society': Jury Is Asked to Sentence Convicted Killer To Death." *Baltimore Sun* (January 28, 1992).

———. "Thanos Guilty on All Counts in Robbery, Slayings." *Baltimore Sun* (January 25, 1992).

———. "Thanos Trial's 'Shock' Value Testimony Starts in Teens' Murders." *Baltimore Sun* (January 24, 1992).

Hit Man Murders

Articles

Bowers, Karen. "A Gruesome Triple Murder Puts a Boulder Publisher and Its How-to-Kill Book in the Crosshairs." *Denver Westword* (March 21, 1996).

Brooke, James. "Lawsuit Tests Lethal Power of Words." *New York Times* (February 14, 1996).

Dean, Eddie. "Hitsville U.S.A." *Washington City Paper* (October 20, 1995).

Hermann, Peter. "Father Arrested in 3 Murders." *Sun* (July 21, 1994).

Jenkins, Ray. "Court Ruling Deals Blow to Free Speech." *Sun* (November 17, 1997).

Jennings, Veronica, and Kevin Sullivan. "Disabled Boy, 2 Women Found Slain." *Washington Post* (March 4, 1993).

Levine, Susan. "Perry Gets Life without Parole in Triple Killing." *Washington Post* (May 17, 2001).

Sullivan, Kevin. "Accused Went from Glamour of Motown to a Life of Modest Means." *Washington Post* (July 21, 1993).

Terman, Linda Miller. "Man Found Guilty in Contract Killings: Hit Man Faces Death Penalty for Triple Murder." *Washington Times* (October 13, 1995).

Vick, Karl. "Anger Tinges Grief for Slain Mother, Son." *Washington Post* (March 7, 1993).

———. "Cousin Says He Was Horn's Middleman." *Washington Post* (April 25, 1996).

———. "Horn Convicted for Three Murders." *Washington Post* (May 4, 1996).

———. "Horn Escapes Death Penalty in Triple Murder." *Washington Post* (May 17, 1996).

———. "Jury in Triple Slaying Told of Search for Untapped Phones." *Washington Post* (September 30, 1995).

———. "Prosecutor Describes a 'Plan . . . So Evil' before Triple-Slaying Case Goes to Jury." *Washington Post* (October 12, 1995).

Wagner, Arlo. "3 Found Dead in Home; Mother, Son, Nurse Killed in Layhill." *Washington Times* (March 4, 1994).

Online Sources

"'Hit Man' Publisher Settles Lawsuit, Agrees to Stop Selling Book," retrieved July 5, 2008. www.freedomforum.org/templates/document.asp?document ID=7332&printerfriendly=1.

"'Hit Man' Publisher Settles Oregon Lawsuit," retrieved July 6, 2008. www.freedomforum.org/templates/document.asp?documentID=15793.

Internet Death Wish

Articles

"Death on the Internet." *Time* (November 18, 1996).

"Internet Sex Killer Dies in Prison." Associated Press (February 19, 2002).

Landers, Ann. "Internet Has Its Good Side, Too." Greensboro, NC, *News & Record* (February 17, 1997).

Nowell, Paul. "Woman Seeks Death on Internet." Associated Press (October 30, 1996).

Scully, Sean. "Accused Killer's Former Wife Is Paying the Price; Hears Whispers on Internet Crime." *Washington Times* (October 14, 1997).

Struck, Doug, and Fern Shen. "Networking with Stranger Was Fatal." *Washington Post* (November 3, 1996).

"Take My Life Please." *News & Observer* (November 3, 1996).

Usborne, David. "Woman Arranged Her Own Sex Murder on the Internet." London *Independent* (October 31, 1996).

"Woman Killed in N.C. Led Secret Sexual Life Via Computer." Associated Press (November 4, 1996).

Online Sources

"All about Sharon Lopatka," retrieved March, 12, 2008. www.crimelibrary.com/notorious_murders/classics/sharon_lopatka/5.html.

"CyberMurder.com: Part I, Bound for Death," retrieved March 12, 2008. http://lifeloom.com/III1Godwin.htm.

"Murder She Wrote, November 12, 1996," retrieved May 5, 2008. www.joabj.com/CityPaper/murder.html.

Beltway Snipers

Books

Cannon, Angie, and the staff of *U.S. News & World Report*. *23 Days of Terror: The Compelling True Story of the Hunt and Capture of the Beltway Snipers*. New York: Pocket Books, 2003.

Horwitz, Sari, and Michael Ruane. *SNIPER: Inside the Hunt for the Killers Who Terrorized the Nation*. New York: Ballantine Books, 2004.

Article

Carter, Mike, Steve Miletich, and Justin Mayo. "Errant Gun Dealer, Wary Agents Paved Way for Beltway Sniper Tragedy." *Seattle Times* (April 29, 2003).

Online Sources

"Beltway Sniper Attacks," retrieved March 24, 2008. www.answers.com/topic/beltway-sniper-attacks.

"The Beltways Snipers' Motives," retrieved March 24, 2008. www.danielpipes.org/blog/82.

"John Allen Muhammad," retrieved February 23, 2008. www.answers.com/topic/john-allen-muhammad.

"Jury Begins Deliberations in Beltway Sniper Case," retrieved March 24, 2008. www.foxnews.com/story/0,2933,197422,00.html.

"Lee Boyd Malvo," retrieved February 23, 2008. www.answers.com/topic/lee-boyd-malvo.

"Sniper Attacks: The Legal Case," retrieved March 24, 2008. www.cnn.com/SPECIALS/2002/sniper.legal.

"Two Men to Share Sniper Reward," retrieved March 24, 2008. www.freerepublic.com/focus/f-news/1102136/posts.

Cat o' Nine Tails

Books

Gambrall, Thomas. *Church Life in Colonial Maryland*. G. Lycett, 1885.

Pleck, Elizabeth Hafkin. *Domestic Tyranny: The Making of American Social Policy against Family Violence from Colonial Times to the Present*. Champaign, IL: University of Illinois Press, 2004.

Articles

Farquhar, Roger B. "The Law of the Lash Dies in Free State." *Washington Post* (August 16, 1953).

"The Whipping Post." *New York Times* (April 4, 1897).

"The Whipping Post in Maryland." *New York Times* (January 13, 1895).

"The Whipping Post in Maryland." *New York Times* (August 27, 1896).

Online Sources

Cox, James A. "Bilboes, Brands, and Branks: Colonial Crimes and Punishments." retrieved 18 November 2008. www.history.org/Foundation/journal/spring03/branks.cfm

"Last Whipping Post Sentence in Cecil County," retrieved April 17, 2008. http://cecilhistory.blogspot.com/2007/06/last-whipping-post-sentence-in-cecil.html.

Executions in Maryland

Books

Duncan, John M. *Travels through the U.S. and Canada, 1818 and 1819.* Glasgow, Scotland: University Press, 1832.

Semmes, Raphael. *Crime and Punishment in Early Maryland.* Baltimore, MD: Johns Hopkins University Press, 1938.

Articles

McMenamin, Jennifer. "State Has Long History of Capital Punishment." *Baltimore Sun* (December 6, 2005).

McMenamin, Jennifer, and Laura Smitherman. "O'Malley OK's Step toward Executions; Governor 'Sadly' Orders Procedures Drafted." *Baltimore Sun* (May 23, 2008).

Mencken, H. L. "On Hanging a Man by the Neck." *Baltimore Evening Sun* (August 16, 1926).

Rich, Eric, and John Wagner. "Maryland High Court Calls Halt to Executions." *Washington Post* (December 20, 2006).

Online Sources

"Capital Punishment History: A Historical Perspective," retrieved March 31, 2008. www.dpscs.state.md.us/publicinfo/capitalpunishment/historical .shtml.

"In Md. Most Want Options of Execution," retrieved June 22, 2008. www.baltimoresun.com/news/local/politics/bal-te.md.poll15jan15, 0,2782691.story.

Charm City—Murder Magnet

Articles

"Baltimore Homicide Rate Drops Dramatically." Associated Press (June 30, 2008).

Ditkoff, Anna. "Murder by Numbers: A Look behind the Sad Statistics of Baltimore's 2005 Homicide Toll." *Baltimore City Paper* (January 18, 2006).

Nuckols, Ben. "Baltimore Reduces Homicides in '08, but Remains Among Nation's Bloodiest." Associated Press (January 2, 2009).

Online Source

Ewalt, David. "America's Most Murderous Cities." Forbes.com. Retrieved 8 November 2007. www.forbes.com/2007/11/08/murder-city-danger-forbes life-cx_de_1108murder.html

Kartalija, Jessica. "Baltimore's Murder Rate Continues to Climb." WJZ-TV (December 31, 2007).

Nuckols, Ben. "Baltimore Homicide Level Spike in 2007." Associated Press (January 2, 2008).

America's Oldest Prison

Book

Shugg, Wallace. *A Monument to Good Intentions: The Story of the Maryland Penitentiary, 1804–1995*. Baltimore: Maryland Historical Society, 2000.

Article

"Baltimore Man Keeps Past Prisoners Alive: He's Unofficial Historian for Oldest U.S. Prison." Associated Press (April 7, 2008).

Online Source

"State Agency Histories at the Maryland State Archives: Maryland Penitentiary," SH-33, retrieved May 23, 2008. http://guide.mdarchives.state.md.us/history.cfm?agency=33.

Acknowledgments

I appreciate the willingness of Kyle Weaver of Stackpole Books to allow me to write this book. This is my second association with him and his company, and once again it has been both enlightening and enjoyable. I also appreciate the excellent work of production editor Brett Keener, who added to the content and quality of this volume.

This book involved significant document research, and I was fortunate to receive suggestions and materials from several well-known and recognized researchers and historians, including Suzy Bell, Cecil County Public Library in Elkton; Dan Bonsteel, Maryland Room of the Enoch Pratt Library in Baltimore; Mike Dixon, Historical Society of Cecil County in Elkton; William Jones and Jeff Korman, Maryland Department of the Enoch Pratt Free Library in Baltimore; Raymond Kight and Darren Popkin, Montgomery County Sheriff's Office in Rockville; Fred Rasmussen, *Baltimore Sun*; Mark N. Schatz, Ann Arrundell County Historical Society in Glen Burnie; and staff in the Research Room of the University of Delaware Hugh M. Morris Library in Newark.

My wife, Kathleen Okonowicz, and my good friend Ted Stegura provided proofreading and content suggestions. As always, their valuable help is appreciated.

If I have neglected to mention anyone from whom I have received assistance during this project, I truly apologize.

About the Author

Ed Okonowicz is a storyteller and a regional author of more than two dozen books on Mid-Atlantic culture, oral history, folklore, and ghost stories. As an adjunct professor, he teaches folklore at the University of Delaware, from which he retired after working for more than twenty years as a writer and editor. His books include short story collections, sports biographies, oral history volumes, and novels. He is the author of *Haunted Maryland*, published by Stackpole Books. In 2005, he was voted Best Local Author in the *Delaware Today* magazine readers' poll. He has appeared on The Learning Channel and on radio and television stations in the Baltimore-Philadelphia region. His website at www.mystandlace.com provides information on all of his books and programs, which he presents for a wide range of audiences in venues that range from schools and colleges to convention halls and historic sites. Contact him at edo@mystandlace.com.